MW00683142

THE FILLING VACANCIES TOOLBOX

A Step-by-Step Guide for Ontario Real Estate Investors
and Landlords for Renting Out Residential Real Estate

By Quentin D'Souza

Copyright © DREIC Publishing 2015

The Filling Vacancies Toolbox

A Step-By-Step Guide for Ontario Real Estate Investors and Landlords for Renting Out Residential Real Estate

Publisher: DREIC Publishing

Copyright Canada, USA & the World 2015

ISBN: 978-0-9936717-2-2

Feedback and Comments: info@theontariolandlordtoolbox.com

THE FILLING VACANCIES TOOLBOX

A Step-by-Step Guide for Ontario Real Estate Investors
and Landlords for Renting Out Residential Real Estate

By Quentin D'Souza

DREIC Publishing

2015

Acknowledgements

Starting off, I'd like to thank my lovely wife Laura, for accommodating all of my ideas and projects. Without her support, I would not have been able to attempt this book or build a real estate portfolio. And I want to send out big hugs and thanks to my boys, Darcy and Lucas.

This book, like my previous, was built on the knowledge of so many other real estate investors, landlords, paralegals, lawyers, real estate agents, and property managers that I have met over the years. I know that these people also garnered their knowledge from other people before them, and so on. It would be impossible for me to give credit to all of you individually, but I do want to thank you.

I wanted to give a very special thank you to Harry Fine of Landlord Solutions. He shared some great notice template resources, when he came to speak at a *Durham Real Estate Investors Club* event. I used his templates as a basis for a number of my own notice templates.

There are so many contributions from people, both big and small, that appear throughout the book. Thank you to the thousands of real estate investors, landlords, and real estate business owners that I have met at the Durham Real Estate Investment Club (DurhamREI.ca).

In particular, I would like to thank Tania Hobbs, Andrew Brennan, Jeff Woods, Ian Szabo, Julie Broad, Tom Karadza, Nick Karadza whose tips, support, and direction has helped me tremendously.

TABLE OF CONTENTS

"*Your present circumstances don't determine where you can go; they merely determine where you start.*"

– NIDO QUBEIN

WHO NEEDS A VACANCIES BOOK?

Why "Investing" Successfully Isn't What You Think

I've been a real estate investor for the past 10 years. Like most, I started small. At first, I wanted nothing more than to improve my chances at a comfortable retirement. In those days, I was a full time teacher. Most people know that teaching is an honourable profession, but it's far from the highest paying. I made pretty good money, my wife also worked, we had kids, and we lived a pretty normal life.

Now, most teachers have a single plan for retirement – to collect pension. Don't get me wrong, pensions are a great idea, and the reasoning behind them is sound. Everyone puts aside a bit of the money they make today, it all gets put into a pool where it can be leveraged into solid investments, and then everyone pulls a bit out for the rest of their lives. We all live happily ever after and there's nothing to worry about. It works perfectly – in theory.

I loved teaching, but there was another part of my brain that couldn't stop thinking – not about how the pension system works in theory – but about the flaws in the pension system. I realized that not all is perfect in pension land, and there are some big questions that could affect my retirement for the worse.

For example, the existing pension system didn't account very well for demographic shifts. I knew that people keep living longer and longer, which means pensions have to pay out longer and longer. In addition, I knew the birth rate worldwide was rapidly dropping. Would there be enough new teachers filling the pension fund on the front end to ensure the coffers stayed full?

Or, what about inflation? Sure, it's great to receive a pension that seems sufficient now for the rest of your life, but what would be the real value of that pension by the time I'm 80? 90? If the pension is not indexed to the inflation rate, and most pensions are moving away from this, the actual value of the money you receive decreases. I plan on living a long time, and every passing year my pension's real value would drop and drop.

Or, what about the investments of the pension fund? The more I looked at the institutional investing system, the more I realized that returns on investment are consistently and relentlessly eroded by fees all throughout the system. If this is happening, how can I even be certain that the pension is being well managed? As a teacher, I had zero say in how they managed the money I put aside every month.

Or, what would happen if public sentiment around defined benefit pensions for government employees changed? I saw what was happening in other provinces, states, and countries, where pensions for those who worked for the government were changing because those governments could no longer afford to pay them. If this could happen in other countries, could it happen in Ontario, Canada as well?

Those were just some of the concerns I wondered about pensions. There was also the question of 'standard investments' that I'd also been led to believe would take care of me. You know what I mean – RRSPs and mutual funds. Yes, I got roped into that world as well. Now, don't get me wrong, there are some solid principles behind RRSPs. It makes sense to avoid being taxed on earnings if possible, but the system of investing in RRSPs is restrictive and is designed to ensure investors lose.

The Turning Point

So, there I was – a teacher concerned about his retirement and financial future. I'm not pretending this is rare. It happens to a LOT of people in any profession or job, but for me it was when I discovered real estate investing was an option to secure my family's financial future in ways that a standard pension plan could not. Eventually, I found the support of other real estate investors, which helped me take great ideas about growing real estate assets, cash flow, and owning businesses, and turn them into practical real estate investing.

Again, I don't think everything in my journey is entirely rare. If you're reading this book, there is a pretty good chance you had a similar journey. I probably don't need to convince you about the power of real estate. If you're reading this book, it likely means you've already discovered real estate in some form. If this is your first introduction to real estate investing, I'd like to welcome you to the wonderful world of real estate, but more importantly, I'd like to commend you on your starting point.

What do I mean by that?

Here's the thing. I've learned a lot during my ten year journey of real estate investing, and that time and experience has taught me some vital lessons. That's what this book is about. I may have started out with the humble goals of improving my chances at a comfortable retirement, but I discovered so many truths and secrets about real estate investing along the way that I have to share this knowledge. We all love real estate investing, but the vast majority of investors continually under-deliver on property management, and it's destroying their chances at success.

As I got better and better at real estate investing, and as I learned more and more from other investors and at conferences and seminars, it became blatantly obvious that the biggest roadblock to success in real estate investing for investors, is sound property management skills.

The big investors have this figured out. They know that systematized, efficient, and effective management is the key to improving cash flows, growing equity, and staying in the game. That last point might sound kind of mundane, but staying in the game is exactly what it takes to get the real benefits of real estate. It's a long-term game, and every year you can hold a property your returns grow exponentially. The big guys know the real secret is staying in it long term, but the small investors don't seem to know it.

We should know it. I mean it sounds easy, right? You just buy lots of properties, then hold onto them forever and end up rich. Or so it seems when we first start. Unfortunately, that's the approach of most real estate education systems. We're led to believe, whether purposefully or not, that the real trick of real estate investing is in acquisition rather than management – but it's not. Now, I'm not saying acquisitions aren't important, but all the great buying strategies in the world will never result in real estate success without being able to manage the properties effectively.

Here's what happens. Investors usually come to the game in a way similar to me. Once they start getting educated, they learn about

- Cash Flow
- Equity Appreciation
- Market Fundamentals
- Special Methods of Acquisition (vendor financing, etc.,)
- How to Use Joint Venture Money

Now, don't get me wrong, all of these are great things. There is no doubt that it's these benefits that result in real estate investors producing unheard of results, especially compared to traditional means of investing that most of us experience first (i.e. mutual funds)However, once investors have learned all about these various aspects of real estate, they are generally fired up and excited. Yet, most new investors don't properly understand the job of landlording, and they certainly don't understand that, above all the exciting components of real estate investing, it's *excellent landlording that provides the greatest ROI (Return on Investment)*.

Now, this might be a controversial statement in some circles. I know for a fact that not everyone agrees with me, and most of those who do only agree begrudgingly. We have a pretty unique club – we who believe that *excellent landlording provides the greatest ROI (Return on Investment)*.

I'm not talking about a literal club here. I'm just talking about individual investors who believe in the power of excellent landlording. I've spent considerable effort over the years building an actual real estate club that honours the importance of landlording as the true golden ticket of this business. It's called the *Durham Real Estate Investment Club (DurhamREI.ca)*. We meet every month. And while we discuss all real estate related issues, we give landlording the attention it deserves because we know the returns landlording can provide.

I know what you're thinking, "Wow, sounds like a boring real estate club." Well, compared to the "pump up" style real estate clubs and seminars that you may have frequently heard of, it might sound boring, but I'll tell you what's not boring – the ROI that our club's investors are seeing. There is no doubt in my mind that top notch property management is the difference between excellent and mediocre results as a real estate investor.

Oh, and in case you're wondering, "What's the big deal? Just hire property managers and be done with it."

I will agree that this would be perfect if it was always possible, but the reality is, it's almost never the best solution for independent investors. If you have a portfolio of single family or small multi-family properties (duplexes and triplexes) then you will have a difficult time finding excellent property management that won't completely eat up your cash flow.

In spite of most real estate educators claims, it's a heck of a lot harder to, "just hire property management" than it seems. For many real estate investors, we will need to manage our properties in the short and medium term.

Why Boring is Important

A few months back, I met an investor named Tom (not his real name). His story is both interesting and somewhat tragic. Not tragic in the sense that people died unnecessarily, but tragic in that a promising real estate career and a family's financial future were sacrificed. I wish I could tell you it's an uncommon story, but it's not.

Tom started his real estate journey much like I described my own above. His story of real estate discovery has some different details, but the basic structure is the same. He too had a good paying job but didn't see the retirement future in it. He also discovered the principles of other real estate investors and joined real estate investment clubs. He also learned about cash flow, joint ventures, economic fundamentals, and growing equity.

He also *didn't* learn property management. I mean *really learn*. Sure, he knew the basics. But he didn't have a solid understanding of property management, so he didn't grasp that buying 18 properties in 3 years without an incredible property management system would be completely unsustainable.

It turned out it was unsustainable, and Tom ended up losing everything.

I'm not prone to overstating the truth, so I'm obliged to provide some context. Poor property management was not the only factor that caused Tom to lose all of his properties when the market took a downward turn. There were other issues.

However, it's not an overstatement to say that property management was one of the biggest factors that brought about his real estate downfall. At the time, he had a 20% vacancy rate when the broader market was closer to 5%. Due to his poor systematization, he found himself getting behind on his bills and not being able to make simple changes to advertising his property which caused vacancy problems at the worst possible moment.

You see, when the housing market makes its inevitable shift to the negative (it happens to every investor if they stay in the game long enough), it's the worst possible time to find out your property management system is lacking.

A far better approach – one that might have saved Tom – is to be obsessed with perfecting your property management system from the first moment you start investing and stay on top of it for the duration of your career. Now, you might be thinking, "I'm not like Tom, I only want to own 5 properties. I could never get behind on my property management like he did."

Respectfully, I'd like to tell you that you're wrong if you believe that. Even if your goals are more modest, property management remains vital. Treating it with a 'mom and pop' mentality is unsustainable. Mom and pops aren't built to last.

You will be frustrated all the time if this is your property management approach because it's not repeatable. When you have to reinvent the wheel every single time a situation arises, you're essentially committing to a lifetime of frustration.

If you don't think 5 properties can be much property management work, then you probably haven't experienced it yet. Even a few properties without an excellent system can begin to seem like an insurmountable task. It leads to burnout. In fact, this problem is far more common than the problems that plagued Tom – even though Tom's story in itself is quite common.

It's gotten so bad that investor burnout is often just thought of as part of the job of being a real estate investor. It's bad because it causes people to stop acquiring new properties, and it happens to investors every single day. This means investors are limiting themselves to smaller goals. Think about it. If you only have a few properties and they cause so much work, then you'd be justified in believing that many properties will be that much more difficult to manage. To a small investor struggling with the management of a few properties, adding more properties will seem overwhelming.

Most investors don't grow as fast as the likes of Tom, so they get to see the problem of property management play out before they pass that invisible threshold where they can no longer manage. Instead, they just stop growing their portfolio and fall out of love with real estate.

This leads them to do one of two things. Some investors sell to get rid of "the headache" of owning investment properties. And others, just stop growing their portfolio choosing to suffer through the holding period.

Now, as long as an investor is happy with the number of properties they have (and the cash flow, equity, etc.,) this notion of just "hanging on" is a problem. Who wants to hate a set of tasks they know they'll have to do over and over again for years and years? That sounds terrible, it doesn't have to be like that.

Property management can be easy, systematized, and in the end, not take much of your time at all. Surprised? Doing it this way is important for combatting all of the problems I just spoke of above.

Take Tom for example. If he had implemented an efficient, effective, and simple landlording system to his real estate investment business, he would have made it through the tough market times as a real estate investor. Having a 20% vacancy rate compared to a 5% vacancy rate was the difference between staying in business or not. In the end, he lost his real estate because of this problem.

The same lesson applies to the multitude of burnt out smaller investors. Systematizing their entire process could mean the difference of millions of dollars in staying power.

This book, along with its companion book, *The Property Management Toolbox: A How to Guide for Ontario Real Estate Investors and Landlords,* is designed to deliver this kind of systematization directly into your hands. If you're like most independent real estate investors, then you will find tons of practical wisdom in this book that you can apply immediately.

I know the advice in this book is excellent for two reasons. First, everything in this book is exactly what I use in my business. I know it works. Because, along with my full time job (I stopped teaching a few years back and started education technology consulting), I've been successfully managing a portfolio that's grown to over 24 properties.

This is an important point. I didn't want to put my property management system in the hands of anyone else unless I was certain it could be used by anyone with a full time job. While many investors dream of real estate investing full time and "living the dream," the reality is that maintaining a job while growing your portfolio is highly recommended for many reasons.

Second, I know the advice in this book is excellent because I've shared it with hundreds of other investors. In fact, much of the advice shared in this book was learned from my fellow investors at the *Durham Real Estate Investment Club* and elsewhere. This book is very much a compilation of best practices about filling vacancies, just as my other book *The Property Management Toolbox: A How to Guide for Ontario Real Estate Investors and Landlords* is for landlording as a whole.

All of my experience as a real estate investor and my experience speaking with and teaching other investors have led me to one conclusion: excellent property management is the deciding factor between the investors that have staying power, and therefore reap all the benefits of real estate investing, and those that don't.

My sole purpose in writing this book is to give you the tools to master the vacancies process, which is a huge part of landlording. This will allow you to stay in the game longer, and potentially make millions more dollars (over the course of your career). This is the point of real estate investing, and it solves the original problem of financial security that brought you to into real estate.

When you're done reading this book, you'll have the tools and the knowledge to immediately improve and systematize the vacancies process. Please don't wait. Start reading today, and implement what you learn immediately. This book has the power to transform your real estate investing from a hobby to a new lifestyle on your own terms. But for that to happen, it has to be read, understood, and implemented. I invite you to get started on that process immediately.

"*Don't judge each day by the harvest you reap but by the seeds that you plant.*"

– ROBERT LOUIS STEVENSON

CHAPTER 1

INITIAL STEPS

A Starting Point

Have you ever jumped into a situation (as a real estate investor) and felt unprepared after the fact? If you've ever felt like this, you're not alone. In fact, this happens to landlords all the time.

This is what's known as, "Mom and Pop syndrome". Don't get me wrong, everyone loves Mom and Pop. They go out of their way to take care of everyone. They give unselfishly, and they're pleasant. Mom and Pop certainly aren't your typical tough-minded landlords.

This is the other landlording stereotype – the gruff, battle-hardened landlord who never gives an inch and makes every tenant feel like a grade 3 student, who just got in trouble for shooting spitballs.

Unfortunately, most landlords think they have to choose between taking on one of those two personas. But this couldn't be further from the truth. There is a middle way, and I call it being a *proactive landlord*.

Now, you might know that being proactive means taking action on a situation before it becomes a problem. This is exactly what I'm going to suggest you do as a landlord. Rather than waiting for a particular landlording situation to come to you, then reacting, I want you to be ready for the problem before it happens. Now, you might be thinking, "How am I supposed to know a problem is going to happen before it happens?"

The answer is that most landlording problems are problems of repetition. Sure, some situations might seem like they're unique, but chances are each situation will arise from a select few recurring problems, so when a problem feels new, it's likely just a variation on a repeat issue.

Vacancies are one of the biggest repeat issues that we face as landlords, and being proactive starts the moment a vacancy arises. This chapter is all about being proactive. In fact, the steps you're about to read about are almost never discussed or carried out by reactive landlords.

In this chapter you'll learn about the steps before jumping directly into vacancy filling mode. You see, reactive landlords jump to start filling vacancies before taking the preparation steps that will be discussed in this chapter, and it leads to some negative results.

For example, vacancies can cause landlord anxiety, which by the way is a precursor to landlord burnout. Does the thought of a tenant leaving one of your properties make you feel nervous? Nobody likes to feel nervous, but if you're like many real estate investors (too many) you might feel this way often. In fact, for many it comes standard with real estate investing.

This feeling is caused by a lack of a workable tenant replacement system in place, which is what makes this chapter so important. From the moment a tenant gives notice, the proactive (and calm) landlord begins implementing a series of steps. These steps unburden the proactive landlord from that nagging feeling of nervousness, and this is exactly the topic of this chapter.

Rather than reacting spontaneously to receiving a Notice to Vacate, a proactive and properly systematized landlord should begin executing a series of steps. These steps should be the same every time. That nervous feeling needs to be replaced by a feeling of readiness or preparedness.

Don't suffer this feeling anymore. Read on to learn, but more importantly take action, and implement this system when you receive a Notice to Vacate from a tenant.

Proactive Landlord Vacancy Filling Rule #1

Always take necessary preparation steps before reacting to a vacancy.

Tenant Gives Notice to Vacate – Start Here?

For the sake of staying as close to the process as possible, I've chosen to start this book at the point of the process when a tenant gives notice to vacate. Now, you might be thinking, "Quentin, my tenant didn't give me notice. I don't even have a tenant. I just bought this property and it's vacant."

If this is your situation just skip ahead to chapter 2. You will need to come back to this section the first time you experience a vacancy, but I recognize that not everyone will be starting with a Notice to Vacate.

However, when this *is* your starting point (which it usually will be over time) it's critical to execute this part of the process correctly. It's critical from the standpoint of filling vacancies, and it's critical to the overall goal of excellent landlording.

If you haven't yet checked it out, I recommend taking a look at another book I wrote called *The Property Management Toolbox: A How to Guide for Ontario Real Estate Investors and Landlords*. There I discuss the entire business and practice of effective landlording. Of all the areas of real estate investing, landlording is the least discussed and the least understood. My goal in both books is to provide a complete reference for landlords to effectively systematize and execute the daily tasks of landlording.

Following Process to Avoid Vacancy

Landlording is a series of processes. Each process requires multiple steps. In this book as well as my other landlording book you'll find that a vital part of each process is the assessment stage. Replacing a tenant is no different.

Proactive Landlord Vacancy Filling Rule #2

Never skip a step in your process.

From the moment a proactive landlord receives the Notice to Vacate he or she must first assess the situation. When carrying out that assessment, the landlord's first order of business is to figure out whether or not the tenant has given the correct amount of notice. Remember that in Ontario, a tenant is required to give at least 60 days' notice when vacating a property.

If the tenant is giving the proper notice of at least 60 days, the next order of business is to make sure that the notice is properly executed. The tenant needs to include a few different things on the notice for it to be valid. These include:

1. Name of tenant
2. Name of landlord
3. Name of property (address)
4. Vacancy date that matches the end of the rental period.

The 4th item on that list is the most important. The tenant must give notice that matches the end of a rental period. For example: the tenant mustn't give Notice to Vacate on the 15th of the June so that they can vacate on the 15th of August if the beginning of the rental period for that lease is on the 1st of the month. If the tenant did give notice on the 15th of June, the earliest they could vacate would be August 31st.

The end of the 60 days' notice must fall the day before a new month's rent would have started, in the case of a monthly rental period. This is vital to properly running your real estate investment business. The proactive landlord takes vacancies and lapses between renters seriously. In fact, I would even say that proactive landlords take these things *personally*.

Only in the most extreme cases should it be necessary to leave a space between renters. Remember that any period of time between renters is time you won't be getting paid. Remember that you're in the real estate business to get paid. Hence, any period of time without getting paid should be considered unacceptable.

I want to stress this point because there are investors out there (and sadly people teaching them) that believe it's unavoidable to experience lapses between renters. This is simply untrue, and anyone who believes this and practices it, just isn't treating real estate as a business. At that level it's more of a hobby.

Now, I'm not suggesting that a lapse will never happen. Even the most proactive and properly systematized landlord in the world will at times deal with an unavoidable circumstance that forces them to leave a property vacant for a time. However, these circumstances are the exception rather than the rule and should be treated as such in the mind of the proactive landlord.

The tenant can only give notice for mid-month if this was the beginning of their rental period on their lease. However, as a landlord you should always aim to start leases on the beginning of a month because it's far easier to fill vacancies at the beginning of a month than mid-month.

Action Steps
- Assess whether or not notice has been properly filed
- 60 days
- Name of tenant
- Name of landlord
- 60 days falls on end of the rental period for monthly leases

N-9 Form vs. N-11 Form

The job of the proactive landlord is to foresee and prevent situations before they happen. Above, I discussed the difference between reacting and executing a series of steps. The best way to minimize risk is to see problems happen before they happen and take preventative measures. This is the definition of being proactive.

You will never be able to prevent every situation that may arise, but there is an extremely high level of care and skill that we are able to execute as landlords. Most landlords are not aware how high this level truly is.

One such problem I've never had to deal with but am prepared for anyway is what might happen if a tenant gave notice and said they were going to vacate a property, but when the time for their vacancy came they decided to stay. This would be a problem if the landlord had already found a new tenant for the property, as the landlord would have an agreement with the new tenant, yet be unable to provide vacancy. This is highly unlikely but it's worthwhile to prepare for such an eventuality.

Most often the Notice to Vacate matches the end of the lease period. The most common form used to communicate from the tenant to the landlord is the N-9 found on the Ontario Landlord Tenant Board Web Site (http://www.ltb.gov.on.ca/en/). This form states that the tenant will be leaving at the end of the rental period.

In 97% of cases this form would be good enough. The tenant gives the form and vacates when the form states they will. However, what would happen if the tenant didn't vacate at that time?

One way to mitigate the risk of this happening is to prepare an N-11 form and have the tenant sign. The N-11 form states that both parties agree that the lease will end on the date stated. In the eventuality that a tenant didn't want to leave when the period ended having he N-11 would allow the landlord to go immediately to the eviction process.

When this form is presented to the Landlord Tenant Board as evidence it becomes a rubber-stamping process. If you do suspect problems with a particular tenant, it could be possible that the Board may question this form, if the tenant does not agree that they signed it. Hence, it is important to document the communication through your email transactions or having another third party witness the signing. Nevertheless, having one on file is a good insurance policy against the original tenant staying past their leaving date and therefore sabotaging the new lease you'd prepared with a new tenant.

The N-9 is usually good enough, but in this odd circumstance it might allow for a bit more leeway to the offending tenant. Thus, having an N-11 form in place is the highest level of risk mitigation.

Tenant Gives Less Than 60 Days' Notice or Breaks Lease

One of the main tasks of the landlord is to train the tenant. This might sound a little bit strange, but I assure you that excellent training can be the difference between a mediocre and excellent tenant. I discuss this idea in much greater detail in *The Property Management Toolbox: A How to Guide for Ontario Real Estate Investors and Landlords.*

You see, many tenants have learned through experience renting properties that they can do almost anything and landlords being so desperate will continue to allow them to take actions that aren't allowed by the Landlord Tenancy Act.

So, we try to educate them by discussing their responsibilities all through the process. When the tenancy starts it's the perfect time to let tenants know that their responsibility is to give at least 60 days' notice when vacating a property.

The property binder (see *The Property Management Toolbox: A How to Guide for Ontario Real Estate Investors and Landlords*) you give your tenants should include explanation and the correct forms to use when giving a Notice to Vacate. Hopefully you've taken that step, but even if you haven't, you'll know that sometimes tenants don't follow the process correctly.

A perfect example of this is regarding the notice to vacate. Tenants often don't follow this process perfectly by giving only 30 days' notice instead of 60 as required. If this happens there are four steps a proactive landlord must take:

1. Begin the normal process to fill vacancy

2. Act as though the property will be vacant in 30 days, and try to fill the vacancy that quickly.

3. Inform tenant that they are obligated to provide 60 days' notice for a monthly tenancy using a letter.

4. Follow-up in a separate letter and explain to the tenant that you will try to work with them by filling the vacancy within 30 days, but that you can't guarantee to do this – in which case they would have to pay one more month of rent.

Less Than 60 Days Notice

Date: April 8th, 20XX

Mr. Thomas Tenant
222 Maple Street
Whitby, Ontario
B2B 2B2

Dear Mr. Tenant:

We are in receipt of your N9 notice of termination dated February 28th, received by me on March 6th, informing us that you will be vacating the unit and terminating the tenancy on April 26th, 2014.

While we are accepting your notice to terminate the tenancy as proof that you intend to move out on that date, your notice is lacking in two respects. First, it does not provide the landlord with 60 days' notice, and second, it is not for the last day of the lease term or of the rental period.

The *Residential Tenancies Act* states the following if notice is not given in accordance with the *Act*:

Arrears of rent when tenant abandons or vacates without notice

88. (1) If a tenant abandons or vacates a rental unit without giving notice of termination in accordance with this Act and no agreement to terminate has been made or the landlord has not given notice to terminate the tenancy, a determination of the amount of arrears of rent owing by the tenant shall be made in accordance with the following rules:

1. If the tenant vacated the rental unit after giving notice that was not in accordance with this Act, arrears of rent are owing for the period that ends on the earliest termination date that could have been specified in the notice, had the notice been given in accordance with section 47, 96 or 145, as the case may be.

Therefore, while we are accepting your notice, rent is still owing until the earliest date that it could have been specified had the notice been properly given. This means that your obligation to pay rent continues until May 31st. 2014, and we will be applying the last month's rent deposit to the month of May, 2014. Accordingly, rent for March and April will be owing as usual.

If you have any questions about your obligation for giving notice and ending a tenancy, please contact the rental office and we will answer any questions you may have.

Sincerely,

Name of Landlord

Breaks the Lease

Date: April 8th, 20XX

Mr. Thomas Tenant
222 Maple Street, Whitby, Ontario, B2B 2B2

Dear Mr. Tenant:

We are in receipt of your N9 notice of termination dated February 28th, received by the office on March 6th, informing us that you will be vacating the unit and terminating the tenancy on April 26th, 2014.

You are in a fixed term lease which ends on June 30, 2014. Therefore the earliest termination date under the *Residential Tenancies Act* would be June 30, 2014.

The *Residential Tenancies Act* states the following if notice is not given in accordance with the *Act*:

88. (1) If a tenant abandons or vacates a rental unit without giving notice of termination in accordance with this Act and no agreement to terminate has been made or the landlord has not given notice to terminate the tenancy, a determination of the amount of arrears of rent owing by the tenant shall be made in accordance with the following rules:

1. If the tenant vacated the rental unit after giving notice that was not in accordance with this Act, arrears of rent are owing for the period that ends on the earliest termination date that could have been specified in the notice, had the notice been given in accordance with section 47, 96 or 145, as the case may be.

Therefore, while we are accepting your notice, rent is still owing until the earliest date that it could have been specified had the notice been properly given. This means that your obligation to pay rent continues until June 3oth. 2014, and we will be applying the last month's rent deposit to the month of June, 2014. Accordingly, rent for April and May will be owing as usual.

However, if you would agree to help us to show the unit by ensuring that the unit shows well and you are flexible on the showings, we will began to search for a new tenant right away, and could possibly end the tenancy sooner.

You would also need to cover some of our advertising costs associated with re-renting the unit, which would be approximately $200-$300.

Sincerely,

Name of Landlord

Review Red Folder

After assessing where you are at regarding the vacancy process (see the above steps) the next step is to immediately pull out the tenant's file and conduct a thorough review of their tenancy. If you follow my advice from *The Property Management Toolbox: A How to Guide for Ontario Real Estate Investors and Landlords* (or use a similar process) you will keep a file for each property that contains all documents pertinent to the property as a whole. Within that file is all of the information pertaining to the specific tenancy.

In my system the folder that deals with all things tenant-related is the red folder. Let's take a look at what's inside the red folder – all of which should be reviewed immediately after the issues about the Notice to Vacate have been resolved:

1. **Review Lease** – The first thing to pull out of the red folder and review in detail is the lease agreement. You goal is to check for any unique clauses that may be included in this specific lease. This might not be an issue when working with only one or two leases, but if your real estate business grows and you end up with multiple properties it quickly becomes difficult to keep track of every detail about every property.

   An example is that you might have a special agreement with a tenant about them paying hydro included in the lease. You need to be aware of this when finding a new tenant so you can inform the new tenant about how the hydro bill will be paid, or you might decide to arrange the hydro differently for the new tenant.

   If you had an agreement in place where the tenant was to pay any differences over and above what was included in the rent now would be the time to become aware of that agreement in order to get any money from the tenant they may owe you.

2. **Review Photos** – Again, if you've followed my system or something similar, you will have taken several photos when the tenant moved into the property.

   Reviewing the photos is important because you want to be fully prepared with the knowledge of the state of the property prior to the tenant's move in.

This is an important step for getting reacquainted with the property.

3. **Review Move-in Inspection Form** – Along with reviewing the photos it's important to review the Move-in Inspection Form in order to be fully up to date about the condition of the property when the tenant moved in. You will soon be doing another inspection of the property for the tenant's move out, so you want to be armed and prepared with the knowledge.

4. **Review All Correspondence** – In my landlording system I recommend channeling all communications through either email or official request forms that the tenant sends you.

   There are several reasons for this. One of the reasons is so that you can develop a paper trail of all communications with the tenant. Having this paper trail gives you unprecedented property knowledge.

   When the tenant moves out you want to know everything that has happened since they've moved in. For example: the tenant may have broken a mirror. In an email conversation they may have agreed to fix the mirror.

   Now that they are moving out you will want to follow up to ensure the mirror has been replaced. If it hasn't you will be able to remind them and ensure they do as promised.

Knowledge is always power in the landlording world. The greater level of knowledge you have about every aspect of the property and about the specific issues with the tenant, the greater prepared you will be. This will allow you to win.

Make Appointment and View Property

After you've surmised that the vacancy is in order and have reviewed the red folder, the next step is to get in to view the property immediately. The purpose of this viewing is to do the move-out inspection.

You have all the evidence of the property's condition based on the move-in inspection, photos, and the correspondence with the tenant. Now you must go to the property as soon as possible to do and discuss the move-out inspection, discuss the showing procedure with the tenant, provide the tenant with move-out forms (if they don't have them or know where to find them in their tenant binder), complete the tenant exit questionnaire, and assess the property condition.

Imagine for a moment the tenant is responsible for some fixes to the property that hasn't yet been taken care of. Would you rather deal with these on the day of move-out, or would you prefer to get in communication with the tenant right away? Advance notice and clear communication is more effective than dealing with things at the last minute or worse yet – having to take the tenant to dispute resolution at the Landlord Tenant Board.

Entering Property After Receiving Notice to Vacate

During the normal run of tenancy it's the landlord's responsibility to give the tenant 24 hours' notice before entering the property. This must be done in writing and must be well documented. After the Notice to Vacate has been received this same rule still applies if entering for an inspection.

However, the rules for entering the property for showings are different. In fact, the landlord doesn't have to give 24 hours' notice to enter the property for a showing, so long as the Notice to Vacate has been given.

I always bunch my showings together so I'm doing several on the same day, which means I generally give my tenants a lot more than 24 hours' notice. Still, there are times when you may want to show a property quickly, in which case it's important to know the rules. This is how the rules for entering after Notice to Vacate are written in Section 26.3 of the Residential Tenancies Act:

A landlord may enter the rental unit without written notice to the tenant to show the unit to prospective tenants if;

a) the landlord and tenant have agreed that the tenancy will be terminated or one of them has given notice of termination to the other;

b) the landlord enters the unit between the hours of 8 am and 8 pm; and

> c) before entering, the landlord informs or
>   makes a **reasonable effort** to inform the
>   tenant of the intention to do so.

Assess Property Condition

The first order of business once the inspection has begun is to assess the property condition. As you will see below, a big part of the move-out inspection is actually tenant communication. There are several items we need to communicate during this time, and they will be discussed below.

One of the most important discussions you will have at this time is explaining the tenant's responsibilities for making repairs prior to their moving out. In order to properly do this it's vital to be prepared with a full assessment (and proof) of the properties condition.

When you sit down with them after assessing the condition you will show them photos of how the property looked with the move-in/move-out form. Do not have this conversation before prior to thoroughly assessing the property condition.

During the assessment, make notes of obvious deficiencies, take photos, and be prepared to explain the difference between normal wear and tear versus property damage. You may also discuss what kind of work can be completed while the tenant is still in the property, such as minor repairs. The following chapter will discuss how to properly execute renovations to avoid vacancy.

Explaining the Showing Process

During this early viewing you'll also explain the process of showing the property. Since you have two months to fill the vacancy it gives you plenty of time to properly show the property. As you will see later in this book, there is a right and wrong way to show a property.

Maintaining an excellent relationship with tenants is vital at all times but never more so than after they've given notice to vacate. The tenant can make your life easy or difficult during this phase by the way they grant access to the property. If they grant access easily, your job of filling the vacancy becomes much easier. If they choose to be disagreeable about granting access, then they can make your job of filling the vacancy very difficult.

However, much of the way the tenant reacts will depend upon you. During this early inspection you have the opportunity to explain that you won't allow showings at any given time. You can explain that showings will be bunched together at specific times to make life easier for the tenant. You can also explain that you will always be there with the potential tenants while showing the property. It's important to tenants that their privacy and security are respected, and there is no better time to reassure them of this than during the inspection.

What to Do if the Tenant Says No to a Showing

One event that could put you in a difficult situation is if a tenant refused to allow showings after they've given Notice to Vacate. As a landlord you don't want even a day of vacancy, and to achieve this you will have to show the property well in advance of the existing tenant's move-out date.

Being understanding and cooperative with the tenant is vital to maintaining a relationship during this critical phase so that nothing happens to jeopardize your ability to show a property.

Legally, the tenant doesn't have the right to deny you to show the property so long as you follow the guidelines mentioned above. However, if the tenant denies your attempts to show, you also don't have the right to just barge into the property. Even though the law is on your side, you don't want to do something this confrontational.

A better strategy is to inform the tenant in advance about their legal obligation to allow you access for showings once the Notice to Vacate has been given. We're always better off when in a teaching position with the tenants rather than a confrontational position. Explain the legal responsibility in advance, and by including the following in your communication: "Impeding entry is an offence under the act and carries a fine up to $25,000 upon conviction. Please feel free to call the Investigations and Enforcement office at 416-585-7214 to learn about your obligations with respect to entry." Using the Municipal Housing Authority's standard will work for 97% of all tenants.

Only 3% of all tenants are what we call in the industry "professional tenants". These rare people are responsible for the vast majority of problems for landlords, and informing them of their legal responsibility doesn't work. We can't be assured of avoiding this type of tenant, but if we practice excellent due diligence when filling a vacancy we can mitigate much of the risk from professional tenants. We will deal with this aspect of filling vacancies later in the book.

In the unlikely event that a tenant doesn't allow showings, the landlord would be put in a very uncomfortable position. The best strategy is to maintain the relationship, as legal recourse would be useless in this scenario. Sure, you might win but you'd never have a resolution before the end of tenancy.

If by some unfortunate turn of events the tenant denies showings, you could try bringing in the Municipal Housing Department. They may be able to convince the tenant that they're in the wrong. However, this solution doesn't hold a candle to retaining the relationship. Do it at all costs, as a good relationship trumps any other aspect of this business.

Move Out Inspection Form

The first order of business during your inspection/ meeting is to do a thorough inspection of the property (see Move Out Inspection Form). You will compare the Move-out Inspection Form against the Move-in Inspection Form (and photos you took) you did with the tenant at move-in time.

Are you beginning to understand the importance of following process? Without those photos and move-in inspection form you have nothing to compare the current state of the property against. With the photos and Move-in forms you have a clear idea of how the property's condition has changed over the tenancy period and proof of those changes.

You will inspect the property thoroughly and fill in the entire Move-out Form before discussing with the tenant. You will also document any repairs necessary or modifications the tenants made to the property with photos.

At the end of your inspection you will sit down with the tenant and go over the items they are responsible for prior to move-out. In some cases you may want to do the work yourself and have them reimburse you (or pay up front). In these cases it's even more important to have proper photos and documentation in case you have to take the case to small claims court.

You will also want to explain the process of small claims court at this time in case the tenant doesn't want to take care of their responsibilities or pay as agreed. Explain that the process requires evidence, that you understand the process well and have evidence, and that you will take the process through to the end, if that means garnishment of wages after a decision in small claims court.

Provide Tenant with Move-Out Forms

There are several forms and documents you will want to provide the tenant with during this meeting. Each of these should already be in the tenant binder you provided the tenant when they moved in. However, there will be a good chance the tenant isn't aware of the forms. Many tenants never look in the binder, and if they do they don't always understand exactly what forms are to be used. In the following paragraphs I will discuss which forms to prepare for the tenant during this meeting.

First is a *Copy of Lease*. The lease is the document that provides a legal basis for the tenancy, so it's important the tenant is aware of any relevant clauses at the time of move-out. Don't just give it to them; discuss it with them before leaving.

Second is a copy of the *Move in/Move Out* form. This is probably the most important form to give the tenants, as it compares the condition of the property prior to move in and at the time the tenant gives notice. When handing them this form it's also the correct moment to discuss the relevant fixes they are responsible for, as this is the document that shows it. Please note that you won't get a tenant's final signature on this until the day of move out. Showing them the form at this time is to better prepare them and set the stage for their responsibilities. Sharing the form early is the best way to show the tenants

Third is the *Clean Up Checklist Form*. Nothing is better than a tenant leaving the property in spotless condition. I will not pretend that you will get this every time, but your odds of success go up when you provide tenants with a form that outlines exactly what they're responsible for upon move-out. I even provide a $50 bonus if all items on the checklist have been fully taken care of. You would be surprised how motivated some tenants get by such a small sum of money. In general, I would suggest this incentive doesn't help with upscale rentals. People who can afford to pay a premium on their rent realize that the 5 hours it takes to scrub and clean the house isn't worth $50 to them. The 'normal' blue-collar tenant is more likely to respond to the incentive, but even with them it's not a guarantee.

However, it's worth a try as the $50 it costs to incentivize cleaning is far less expensive than the $150 you will likely spend to bring in a cleaning service. This will be discussed more below.

Last is the *Tenant Utilities Information Release Form*. This is a form I have all my tenants sign when they first move into the property. It simply states that for whatever reasons, it is necessary that I will be able to speak to the utility companies about the utilities. You may remember from *The Property Management Toolbox: A How to Guide for Ontario Real Estate Investors and Landlords* that the best strategy is always to have the utilities under your tenant's name.

This puts the onus on them to pay their utilities bill and reduces the likelihood of you being stuck paying. However, if the bill is in the tenant's name the utility companies won't generally speak directly with you about the tenant's utilities account unless you have written approval from the tenant. So, the best practice is to get the tenant to sign off on a letter that states the landlord may look at the utilities whenever you need to. This is particularly important at the end of a tenancy, so that one tenant ends their utility payment and the other one begins.

Clean Up Checklist Form

Date:_____

Tenant Information

Name: _____

Address of Rental Unit: _____

_____

Thank you for your stay and we understand that you will be moving out of the above rental property soon. According to the terms of our rental agreement, you will have to leave the rental property in a clean, tidy and damage-free condition.

The following is a list of tasks that you have to carry out before your tenancy ends:

- Remove all your personal items and belongings from the property
- Wash and clean up the interior of the property including the flooring, walls, windows and carpets
- Tidy up the garden and lawn of the property. This includes trimming the grass and removing any weeds.
- Clean up all the appliances and furniture in the property
- Move any furniture and appliances that are out of place to their original positions
- Dispose of all food, trash and unwanted items in the property
- Repair any damages that are caused by your neglect or abuse. If anything is left unrepaired, please inform us in writing

Please make sure that the above tasks are
performed by _____. (dd/mm/yy)
If you need help in this matter, please feel free to
contact me at _____.

Sincerely,

Name of Landlord

Complete Tenant Exit Questionnaire

Depending upon the tenant you may also want to
complete a *Tenant Exit Questionnaire* at this time. If the
tenant was an excellent one, it is a good idea to do a tenant
exit questionnaire. But if they were a troublesome tenant
you won't want to bother with the questionnaire.

This doesn't have to be a written questionnaire that
the tenant's complete, it could be questions that you ask
tenants, while discussing with them the process of showing
the property to prospective tenants.

The reason for distinguishing between good and bad
tenants is that the questionnaire is designed to either
retain or ask for referrals from the tenant. Since you don't
want to retain or get referrals from a bad tenant there is no
point in doing the questionnaire with them

Start the questionnaire by determining what the
tenants' next step is. Are they moving because they have
bought a home? Are they moving for a job or another
inflexible reason?

Once you determine what they're doing next and why they're moving, the next step is to see if you can resolve their issue. It may seem too late at the time they give Notice to Vacate, but often the tenants provide this simply because they don't believe their issue is resolvable. If you show you can resolve the problem, you may be able to retain the tenant. Of course, resolving the issue must be within reason. If resolving the issue requires a big expense or effort on your part you may find it's not worth trying to resolve.

> **Proactive Landlord Vacancy Filling Rule #3**
>
> *Always take care of tenant relationships.*

In some cases you won't be able to resolve the issue that's causing them to move out, but you may be able to entice them to move into another of your properties. Sometimes tenants need a bigger or smaller property depending on their family situation at the time. If you've had a great relationship with them and you also have a property that would fit their next move, why not have them move into another property, if available. The same can be said for location. Perhaps you have another property closer to where they want to move.

If the tenants are excellent but there's nothing you can do to keep them, you can see if they have a referral. Great tenants usually have great friends, so this is exactly the kind of referral you're looking for. I often offer a reward incentive for a great tenant referral and during the time of the tenant questionnaire is the perfect time to offer this incentive.

How Can I Help You?

There's every chance that you will not be able to keep the tenant. After all, they're likely leaving for a good reason. If you've been an excellent landlord they probably don't have much to complain about. Still, it's your job to find out.

The exit questionnaire is a chance to potentially gain some benefit for yourself and your business – by retaining or relocating the tenant, but there is a deeper reason we practice this habit. It's about seeking to take care of others' needs at every opportunity and the side benefits that come along with that.

In reality, all business comes down to this question, "How can I help you?" Once you know someone's needs, you may be able to help – even if only in some small way. For example, if the tenant is leaving your property to buy a home perhaps you can refer an excellent mortgage broker, real estate agent, or contractor.

On the first level, these people will appreciate your referrals. What's better than helping someone who has already helped you? That feeling alone is the proper feeling to remain in when doing business. It reminds us that our efforts are bigger than ourselves. On the self-interested side (and there's nothing wrong with taking care of our own interests) it creates nothing but good will.

Those people you refer today will be more likely to refer tenants and property deals to you. Plus they will feel a higher sense of obligation to treat your situation with the highest level of care, and on top of that, you may even have a direct relationship of receiving referral fees.

If you are already a Realtor, you could get a referral fee just for speaking with a departing tenant for 10 minutes. They may be moving to another town, so why wouldn't you? By finding out where they are considering moving to, and contacting a Realtor in that location, you could negotiate a referral fee on a single deal. It's like free money – just for doing the right thing. If you aren't a Realtor you might be taken out for a nice dinner or show, or perhaps given a sizeable gift card for referring a new client to them.

Being a successful landlord is a balance between taking care of the tenants and taking care of the bottom line. When you go the extra mile to carry out an exit questionnaire you have the chance to take care of both sides of the landlording equation. All by asking that simple question at the heart of all business, "How can I help you?"

Showing Ready Checklist

Once you complete the above-mentioned steps of the preparation phase, then you're ready to dig out the Showing Ready Checklist (find it on www.theontariolandlordtoolbox.com).

I'll discuss this checklist several times in the next chapter, but I'd like to mention here that the purpose of the checklist is to have a standard process for ensuring that you hand over properties to new tenants in a systematized and repeatable way.

Having a repeatable standard ensures that you don't slide back. This phenomenon is known as 'shifting expectations' and it's deadly to landlords everywhere. It happens when a property gets a bit rundown from a tenant. You might be upset and do everything in your power to improve the state of the property, but the next time it happens you might be a little more used to it and lower your standard.

After a while, your standard gets lower and lower until your standard is almost non-existent. The next thing you know, your property is just plain rundown, and you've become a 'tired landlord', or a 'slumlord', or a 'burnt out landlord'. These are all the same title used for landlords whose standards have slid down. There is great danger in this – for both your ability to stay in the game, your cash flow, and your future equity growth.

Having a rent-ready checklist ensures you don't fall prey to sliding expectations syndrome. When you pull out your Showing Ready Checklist at the end of the preparations phase, the first thing you'll need to check off is whether or not renovations are required. If so, then you will initiate your renovations procedure, which is the topic of the next chapter.

Sneak Peak

You just learned about all of the preparatory steps that the proactive landlord takes before jumping into the vacancies filling phase. Each of the steps discussed in this chapter is vital, but would you believe that there is still more preparation?

Being prepared is great, but a proactive landlord will also continually improve her property so that the asset is always maintaining and improving its value, as well as, being in tip top shape to continually attract only the best tenant. And that's the topic of the next chapter.

A lot of landlords get stuck on this problem. They think that if they are to do any renovations they will have to leave the property vacant for a time. I couldn't disagree with this more. Our goal as a proactive landlord is to never leave the property vacant for a day.

This can be tricky to juggle, but it is absolutely vital to your success as a landlord. Read on to the next chapter to see how proactive landlords continually upgrade and renovate their properties without suffering unnecessary vacancies.

" Start where you are.
Use what you have.
Do what you can.

– ARTHUR ASH

CHAPTER 2

RENOVATIONS AND CLEANING PHASE

The Renovation Puzzle Piece

Have you ever struggled to execute every step of a consistent plan? Or have you ever fallen prey to the shifting expectations phenomenon? If so, you're not alone.

What you just learned about stopping, making an assessment of the vacancies situation, and then executing a series of preparation steps (before moving onto the next stage of the vacancies filling process) is vitally important.

It's an advanced step used only by the most proactive landlords. You see many of our landlording brothers and sisters are driven by their fears and anxieties, making rash decisions without proper preparation.

It drives them to skip the first preparation stages of the process, but it can also cause landlords to skip this next all-important phase. The anxiety can cause them to skip the phase that will be discussed in this chapter and ultimately lower their expectations.

The initial assessment and preparation are vital, but this second phase of renovation and cleaning (which can be thought of as a secondary preparation phase) is equally important. In fact, the first phase will be meaningless unless you can get this secondary phase right. Each of the stages of the vacancies filling process can be thought of as another piece of the puzzle. The first phase (discussed last chapter) works only when used with all the other phases, including the renovations phase, which we'll discuss in the next chapter.

Rushing through or failing to execute this second phase properly will defeat your earlier efforts. As always, stick with the system and watch your results improve.

Renovation Work Required

From the moment you receive the Notice to Vacate your job is to do everything necessary to get the property rented out as quickly and efficiently as possible. This does not mean reacting on a whim.

Rather (as you can see from chapter 1), it means instigating a series of repeatable steps to ensure that you don't just get *any* tenant in the property. Instead, you want to get an *excellent* tenant in a properly cleaned and renovated property without a day's vacancy. Oh, and you want to get that kind of tenant near the top of the rental market (in terms of income).

As you can imagine, this takes a bit of a balancing act. How does one do every step properly without a vacancy? It starts with the steps outlined in the Chapter 1, but the real trick begins when it comes time for renovations. You might only have 1 day to handle the renovations before the next tenant moves in, and sometimes it will take all of your care and skill to even get a day.

Legally, the outgoing tenants have until midnight on the day the lease expires. So there's nothing you can do if they choose to push their move until the minute before midnight on the end of the month. However, by being prepared, communicative, and following the process a proactive landlord can avoid vacancy probably 90% or more of the time. How is this possible when the tenant leaving has every right to stay until the last moment? Two things happen.

First, you may be able to come to some kind of verbal agreement with the leaving tenant where you can either ask them to leave at a specific time or allow you to start renovations while they're still there. You'd be amazed at what communication and incentives can do.

Second, there is every possibility the tenant won't be able to leave early. This is easy to understand, as there's a good chance the new place they're moving won't be available until the same day they're vacating your property. If their new property isn't available, it's a big request to ask them to park all of their belongings in a neutral location for a day just so you can renovate the property. Or worse yet, to bring in your crew to renovate while they're still moving.

Please note that even if this is the case, you still don't have to suffer vacancy. Just as you used excellent communication with the outbound tenant you also use excellent communication with the inbound tenant to explain that the renovations will be ongoing for the first day as they move in. Or in the best-case scenario, they may be able to delay moving in while you renovate. The key is that you must get your renovations done right away, usually within the first day.

You'll find that most inbound tenants will be okay with a day of renovations if it means having a nicely spruced up property. It's critical to communicate this to your tenants. A great strategy is to show a sample of the new carpeting or laminate that will be installed in the property when showing or signing the lease. Explain to the incoming tenants that you take renovations seriously, and that your goal is always to have a sharp and professional property. This means you regularly renovate but that it requires the cooperation of the incoming tenant.

Consistently renovating is key because you don't ever want too many renovations taking place during one turnover. If this happens there's a good chance it will take too long and result in a bad relationship with the new tenant.

With normal wear and tear you can expect to replace flooring, paint the walls, change fixtures, and change closet doors quite regularly. Exactly how often you have to do these basic renovations will depend entirely on the tenants leaving as they may or may not cause a lot of damage in the normal run of tenancy.

Doing the Renovation Preparation

One of the most important things you can do for ensuring a smooth renovation process is to execute excellent preparation. In the previous chapter we discussed a different kind of preparation, but for the purpose of this conversation we mean a) assessing which renovations are necessary, and b) getting into the property before the tenant leaves to take care of any renovations possible before the outgoing tenant leaves.

As a proactive landlord, you must make your assessment immediately in order to be able to execute efficient renovations. Part of that assessment will tell you if you can do any early renovations while the outgoing tenant is still in the property. Usually, we focus on the small things that will make the bigger renovation process smoother.

Obviously, you won't be able to paint or install new flooring while the previous tenant is still in the property, but you can patch walls, change out closet doors, install backsplashes, and do other small jobs that don't interrupt the tenant's life.

By having all of these done before the tenant ever leaves, allows you to focus all of your crew's energy on the big tasks like painting and installing flooring during the time allotted.

The rule of thumb is that any renovation that doesn't interrupt the outgoing tenant's life will be allowed. Otherwise, you will need to do it after they leave, but even when assessing these bigger renovations (that can't be done until the tenant leaves) much preparation work can be done in advance – this preparation can drastically improve your ability to deliver smoothly on the renovation.

For example, all flooring must be measured, ordered, and the renovation plan completed. Also, as we'll discuss below it's vitally important to have your team ready for go day. A tradesperson showing up a day late can destroy your process entirely.

To make your assessment correctly, you will have to know exactly what kind of renovations you will be doing. To figure this out, you must understand your tenant profile and renovate to the tenant profile.

Renovate to Tenant Profile

The biggest mistake I see landlords make over and over again is over-renovating. I can't stress enough how vital it is to renovate to the correct level, as spending too much money on renovating the wrong property, is a complete waste of money.

Remember that every property you manage is an *investment*. This means that every dollar you spend on the property is also an investment – directly when you purchase the property and indirectly when spending money on the property in any other way. You must regularly reinvest in the asset in order to maintain the value of the asset. This is true in any business, whether we see the reinvestment or not. Real estate is no different.

However, there isn't a direct correlation between the dollars you spend on a property and the maintenance of its value. Getting the renovations puzzle right is a Goldilocks scenario. Spending on renovations has to be just right – not too much and not too little.

It would be more effective to spend money on the capital costs for the property rather than on high-end touches. Eventually you will have to spend money on capital costs like roofing or a boiler. If you're going to spend thousands of dollars on the average blue-collar property you will get a far better return on investment by spending on these big-ticket non-optional items.

Granite Countertops – Are You Serious?

I like granite countertops as much as the next guy, but I like them in my own home. Or if they are going to be in a rental property, it has to be a property with a high-end tenant profile. Think Dinks (double income, no kids) in downtown Toronto or other metropolitan city (or hippies or hipsters or whatever they're called these days – am I showing my age?) These tenants expect and demand high-end features in any property they may rent.

The key is getting it right. I've seen several real estate investors install granite countertops in average rental properties and it always leaves me shaking my head. There is no possible way to recoup the investment of the granite, as this renovation won't allow you to raise the rents sufficiently enough to cover the cost of the materials and installation. To make matters worse, there's a chance that the fancy countertops will even get damaged – necessitating another renovation soon.

The average tenant does not expect granite, and by giving it to, you're not doing them or yourself any favors. The same could be said for several high-end renovations like hardwood flooring, stainless steel backsplashes, expensive lighting, glass tiling, fancy cabinets, etc. Of course, this will always depend on the tenant profile, and the type of property that you are renting.

Learn the skill of renovation the Goldilocks way and you will always protect and enhance your investment. With my particular tenant profile, the road to long term real estate riches isn't paved with granite countertops, stainless steel, or glass tiles.

Building a Renovation Team

In *The Property Management Toolbox: A How to Guide for Ontario Real Estate Investors and Landlords* I discuss team building in more detail, but it's worth noting here the importance of building a team of handymen and contractors.

Putting together and polishing your power team is an ongoing process, and as long as you're proactive you'll be finding, trialing, and adding new people to your team. You need operational redundancy to ensure you never go without a great tradesman, handyman, or contractor. The moment your tenant gives Notice to Vacate is not the moment to begin building a power team. Start this process the moment you become a landlord and never stop.

You can find great contractors in many ways, but hands down, the best way is through referrals from other landlords. There is no perfect contractor just as there is no perfect person, but success and reliability leave clues. The most reliable clue is the good word of others you trust. The point to understand is that you must build the team in advance in order to set yourself up for success when you receive a Notice to Vacate.

With that warning aside I have to break some bad news to you: even if you build a solid power team of contractors in advance, there's a good chance you will sometimes find yourself using a brand new contractor to renovate a property during a tenant transition. It only makes sense given that you are constantly adding new people to your team, and how do you add them without at least giving them a trial run.

In fact, a time of small renovations like a tenant turnover might be the perfect time to give them a trial run to see how prompt and professional they are. If this is the case, make sure you prescreen the contractor before bringing in any new contractors.

I will even use two new contractors in a property at the same time. In this circumstance both will know the other is there. I don't tell them they're in competition for my future business, I simply tell them I've hired someone else who will be working alongside them due to a time constraint. When you only have one day to get all of your renovations done it's important to do them efficiently.

Give your contractor plenty of notice and explain to them the importance of timing. They need to know that your renovation has to be done on the day you state due to the new tenant moving in. Failure to get it done that day could put you in a sticky situation. Nothing is more important than timing.

Covering Your Ass(ets)

One of the biggest new commitments that Ontario landlords have is to ensure a contractor, who employs other people and is working on your property, is insured with WSIB. Failure to do this could lead to being sued for up to $100,000 if a worker is hurt. Therefore the burden of proof is on us now to ensure anyone working under our roofs is up to snuff.

The process here is simple, but vital. Any contractor you might hire must provide you with a WSIB number. Check their identification to ensure they are who they say they are, and then cross reference the WSIB number on the website to make sure they are up to date and in good standing with WSIB.

Only once you've verified that the contractor is covered you can bring them into the property to commence work.

Line Up Your Renovation and Cleaning Team

You've now completed your preliminary process of the filling vacancies process, and you've lined up one or more contractors. So, how do you prepare the team for the big day? The goal of landlording is always to systematize.

Almost everything you do once as a landlord is something you'll do again one day.

Finding and filtering contractors is one part of the system. The next component is to properly prepare the contractor or handyman. Eventually you will find 1 or 2 trusted contractors or handymen that are perfect for vacancy turnover renovations. Even they might not last forever. People move, people get divorced, they have other projects on the go and life happens.

If you're using the same contractor over and over this process will seem routine after a while and they will know what you want due to repetition. However, even a first time contractor will know exactly what you want. They will know because you will send them your *Showing Ready Checklist* in advance and they will see it on the walkthrough.

I don't recommend you spend your own time cleaning a property when filling a vacancy. In a pinch I've done this at times, and you will likely have to as well. However, a far better strategy is to have a cleaning team or service. I have both. What's the difference?

Chances are you won't have enough cleaning projects to keep a full time cleaner employed unless you own a hotel. This is not what I mean by having a cleaning team. I'm lucky enough to have cultivated an excellent relationship with a painter who does the final cleaning (when the tenant doesn't finish it themselves, which is most of the time).

It started when I brought him in to paint a property. I always have the Showing Ready Checklist on site, and I make sure that each contractor (if there is more than one) knows which of the responsibilities on the showing ready checklist are theirs. On the Showing Ready Checklist are *all* of the tasks required to have a property ready for rent (see website for Showing Ready Checklist). It includes things like replacing smoke alarm batteries, change furnace filters, renovations, and cleaning.

As a landlord this checklist is your standard process for how you will *always* rent a property to the next tenant. Having this process in place ensures your properties don't end up slowly deteriorating year after year. It gives you a standard to achieve. Please note that the Showing Ready Checklist isn't a complete list. From time to time you will have to do other renovations not on the checklist. Assessing those renovations is a different task.

As I was showing my painter all of his job requirements he noticed the cleaning component of the showing ready checklist. I knew him as a painter, so it never crossed my mind to ask him to clean the property. However, when he saw the cleaning tasks on the list he asked me what my plan was to get the cleaning done. I told him I had a cleaning service booked to come in as soon as he was done. He mentioned that his wife does cleaning and that she could come and clean the property while he was painting it and that I could add the fee to his bill. I was thrilled because it simplified my process and I saved a bit of money by using the same person/team to do both jobs.

You may not be so lucky as to find a cleaner/painter in one, but I think of mine as my in-house cleaning team. If you don't have the same luck, it's imperative that you have a cleaning service ready to take care of your property.

The cleaning service must be prompt and efficient. Again, use the Showing Ready Checklist as a guideline for a cleaning service to ensure the property is cleaned to your specifications.

Whether or not you use a cleaning service or an in-house team the most vital part of the cleaning process is to have your cleaners arranged in advance. The same rule applies with contractors. The window for turning over the property is tiny, and there is no room for scrambling. Not having someone booked in advance will cause you great stress. If a cleaner or cleaning service doesn't show up when they promised that's a good reason never to use them again because it sabotages the tenant turnover process.

Team Building – The Secret to Getting it Done

Contractor relationships are nearly as important as tenant relationships. Both tenants and contractors often have bad reputations for being unreliable, but the reality is that there are good and bad (tenants and contractors).

Just as you apply a systematic approach to choosing tenants (which we'll discuss below), so you also apply a systematic approach to choosing contractors. In addition, you must protect your interests by setting up a pay structure with your best interests at heart. This topic is discussed in detail in *The Property Management Toolbox: A How to Guide for Ontario Real Estate Investors and Landlords.*

As a landlord you have to be careful, especially at the beginning, but once a mutual foundation of trust has been established, the relationship can really flourish. I have contractors on my team that I trust implicitly.

This is very important when the renovation turnaround time could be as short as one day. If a contractor shows up one day late it can really mess up my tenant turnover period. I have to trust my team in order to get it done right.

On the flip side, my team needs to be able to trust that I will set them up for success by making sure their tasks are manageable within the time frames I've asked of them. If I throw an unreasonable amount of work at them too many times they will lose their trust in me as a leader.

Nobody likes to work under unreasonable pressure, least of all contractors. I urge you to apply systematic thinking to your renovations process, but remember that relationships trump systems. Do everything in your power to nurture and maintain the relationship, and you will find yourself with smoother renovations than ever before.

Showing Ready?

As mentioned, the Showing Ready Checklist will be the guideline for the renovation team as well as the cleaning team. Often when doing a tenant turnover there will be some small items to repair. These likely won't be the job of the painter or the cleaner, unless you make a specific arrangement with them and if they're capable of the small fixes.

I recommend having a couple of useful handymen on your team. These are the people that can do the smaller kinds of jobs and have made a business of efficiently fixing unique and routine small problems. You might need a toilet or faucet replaced or some trim put in place. A great handyman can do this kind of job.

There's a good chance your handyman will be at the property before the tenant turnover anyways, which makes the handyman the perfect person to carry out much of the Showing Ready Checklist tasks. They can change the batteries in the smoke alarm, change the furnace filters, and all of the other small tasks on the Showing Ready Checklist.

Remember that the tenant is our client, and a proactive landlord's goal is to impress the tenant. This is good business. The more small things you can do to please and impress your tenant the more referrals you get from them, the longer you retain them, and the more goodwill you build with them.

The Showing Ready Checklist ensures you give your tenants an excellent impression from the moment they walk into the property. Remember when you've selected a tenant you will be performing a tenant move-in inspection with them (we'll cover this below). During that walkthrough you will be doing all of the little items like checking the smoke alarms, demonstrating the new paint, and explaining the furnace filter changing procedure.

Not having your own Showing Ready Checklist finished means being embarrassed during the move-in inspection.

This doesn't provide a great first impression, and your tenants will notice. The closer you stick to the landlording process the better business goes over the long term.

Assessing Work to Be Done

It's important to have a minimum standard for tenant turnovers, but there is always other work that *could* be done to a property time permitting. A proactive landlord will always strive to have every property fully rented with no vacancies, but there will inevitably be some turnovers where you're left with a month's vacancy.

This may seem like a defeat, but if it does happen to you there is still a way to salvage the situation. This is the time to *take care of renovations you normally wouldn't have time for on a quick tenant turnover.*

Asset and time management are two big components of property management. A property vacant for a month provides a rare opportunity to manage your asset well and use time efficiently. Prepare and push for no vacancies, but when stuck with a month's vacancy make sure you're prepared with the capital in place to improve the property where needed.

Keep a running list of projects for each of your properties that require longer time to complete, such as replacing the flooring in a property, a gap in vacancies would be an excellent time to do those projects than a short turnover would normally permit.

If "Cleaning Only" Required

From time to time you will experience a vacancy turnover where no renovations will be required. Alternatively, you might have some renovations, but they may be tiny renovations that you can complete before the leaving tenant departs.

Both scenarios mean only cleaning is required between the moment the departing tenant leaves and the moment the new tenant arrives. This is a perfect opportunity to offer the departing tenant the agreement we discussed above (a $50 incentive to clean the property to clean up to rent ready standard).

Or, you may want to arrange a special circumstance agreement. Perhaps the leaving tenant will clean to your rent ready standard in exchange for an extra day or two in the property. Or, perhaps the incoming tenant will do the cleaning in exchange for arriving a day early.

Keep in mind that even if you have a special agreement in place with a tenant for cleaning, you still must complete the non-cleaning portions of the Showing Ready Checklist. Never let tenants complete the Rent Ready Checklist, as there are items in that checklist that affect your liability (smoke alarms working, etc.). Also, ensure that any days that you are allowing a tenant access to your property that they are included in your lease.

Pre-Book Appointments

We've been discussing all of the elements required to hand over a property to a new tenant in a rent ready state. This can be thought of as your landlording baseline, and we've just discussed all the components of carrying out this process.

However, we must be careful not to focus only on the renovating and cleaning required to bring the property to a rent ready state. A proactive landlord will also be pre-booking showing appointments all while the renovations and cleaning process are underway.

Attracting new tenants to the property begins as soon as you've surmised that the outgoing tenant has properly filed their leaving papers, and it doesn't end until the new tenant has signed the lease and paid 1st and last month's rent.

Keep in mind that when showing the property at earlier phases it might not show very well since the renovations and cleaning won't be done, and the previous tenants belongings are likely still in the property. When this is the case, communication is key. You must take sincere effort to explain how things will be different once the renovations are complete and how it will look after the renovations. It's always a good idea to display samples of the carpeting that will be installed and paint that will be applied.

For the purposes of this book we've dealt with the renovations and cleaning phase before a thorough discussion of the marketing and showing phase. However, the reality is that these two phases overlap each other on the tenancy turnover timeline. The next couple of chapters will deal with the marketing component of the process.

> **Proactive Landlord Vacancy Filling Rule #4**
> *Always market your property from the moment you know about an upcoming vacancy.*

Where We're Going

We just finished discussing the various steps of the renovation phase of the vacancies filling process. You should now have an understanding of assessing, planning, and executing the renovations on properties being turned over to new tenants.

As briefly mentioned in the last chapter, this process must be ongoing while also marketing your property to find new (highly qualified tenants). The vacancy filling system is step by step, but the renovation and rental preparation/ marketing steps must (by circumstance) be carried out at the same time.

In other words, it's important that you read and understand the upcoming chapter so that have a great understanding of marketing (and therefore filling) your vacancy while carrying out the maintenance (renovations). Without understanding the marketing system you will sabotage the great efforts you made during the renovations phase, so read on to learn how to carry out the all-important process of tenant attraction.

You have everything you need to build something far bigger than yourself.

– SETH GODIN

CHAPTER 3

RENTAL PREPARATION, MARKETING, AND SHOWING

Intro

Have you ever been slightly (or extremely) mystified or overwhelmed by the idea of marketing? When we look at glossy magazine ads or fancy online marketing campaigns it's easy to think marketing is a special skill that the average person will never master.

Well, this might be true when discussing corporate marketing or some of the more convoluted online marketing methods, but luckily it's not so bad when marketing simple rental properties. In fact, there's nothing to be scared of at all, and best of all, the marketing component becomes a lot easier just by being a proactive landlord. Why is this?

Unfortunately, there are so many reactive (and downright lazy) landlords out there that you will stand out as remarkable just by following the simple steps in this book (and those in my other book *The Property Management Toolbox: A How to Guide for Ontario Real Estate Investors and Landlords*).

It suddenly becomes a lot easier to market a property and attract the exact tenant you want once you have a property that speaks for itself – which you will have when you follow the excellent process discussed above.

Great properties market themselves, so the steps mentioned in the previous chapters are vital to attracting quality tenants, yet there are some simple secrets for marketing rental properties that can make all the difference to a simple tenant attraction process and a convoluted one.

This chapter fills those gaps. Read on to discover the simple but successful tenant attraction strategies of proactive landlords.

Rental Comparable Worksheet

Before we can properly market a rental property we must first get the rental rate correct. The reason for this will be discussed below when we delve into marketing the property. The system for figuring out the correct rental rate to set comes from the rental comparable worksheet.

Rental Comparables Worksheet <<Insert Property Name>>				
Address	**Type**	**Bed/ Bath**	**Advertised Rental Amount**	**Notes/ Comments**
<<Address-Comparable Property #1>>	Insert Type	3/ 1.5	$1,200	<<Insert comments>>
<<Address-Comparable Property #2>>	Insert Type	3/1.5	$1,250	<<Insert comments>>
<<Address-Comparable Property #3>>	Insert Type	3/1.5	$1,300	<<Insert comments>>
<<Address-Comparable Property #7>>	Insert Type	3/ 1.5	$1,300	<<Insert comments>>
<<Address-Comparable Property #8>>	Insert Type	3/ 1.5	$1,395	<<Insert comments>>
Range		**$1,200**	**$1,395**	
Median			**$1,300**	
Average			**$1,289**	
Your Property				
<<Insert Property Name>>			**$1,350**	<<Insert comments>>

Completing the worksheet, and therefore understanding the market rent requires research, and as always executing here is a matter of preparation. In other words, the best time to start researching rental amount for your property isn't when a property becomes vacant. Rental market analysis is an ongoing job in this business. A proactive landlord always knows what his or her properties should be renting for.

In fact, this is one of the biggest errors real estate investors make over the years. Reactive landlords seem to believe that it's easier to let property maintenance and rents slide over the years. Of course, this has far-reaching consequences, one of which is that the tenant profile slides along with the maintenance and the rents.

However, the problems don't start there. This kind (and any kind) of lazy landlording eventually results in the degradation of the value of your asset. This is not a wise strategy considering most real estate investors want to rely on their assets to fund their retirement.

Don't be that landlord.

Part of the task of continuing to be a proactive landlord rather than a lazy landlord is keeping up on market rents. This should be done every 6 months, however if you haven't done one in a while and therefore aren't certain what you should be charging for rent, you can figure it out right away. There is no need to not know what the rents should be for a given property.

If you don't know how much your property should be renting for on the day your tenant gives you notice the best thing to do is immediately start scanning the

Kijiji, Craigslist, and *Rentometer* websites to find out what comparable properties are renting for. The rental stock found there is the best indicator of current rental values because the market is testing these properties. The market rent is just whatever the available renters will support, so there is no more accurate barometer of rental rates than what's currently available online.

It's simple a matter of finding properties that have as many similar features as your property as possible and setting your rental rates at a similar rate. Look at how many bedrooms the property has, how many bathrooms, how many square feet, where the property is, and what kind of shape it's in. The comparables don't have to be perfect to get a good idea, either.

If you find a 3-bedroom, 3-bathroom townhouse only half a block from your 3-bedroom, 2-bathroom townhouse that's renting for $1200 per month you will have a pretty good idea of what your 3-bedroom, 2-bathroom townhouse will also rent for. In this case it would probably be identical as long as they're in similar types of complexes and one isn't in far superior shape.

Please note that 'market rent' is simply what the market will bear. There is no real price for rent. God doesn't ordain these things. They shift as the market demand shifts. Renters are always the best judges of what the market will bear. Keep this in mind because market rents can (and do) change very quickly. Unfortunately, a lot of landlords just set their rents far too low.

This may not seem like a big deal. After all, you may reason that at least having a lower rent price attracts tenants quickly, so maybe it's not so bad. There are two problems with this. First, attracting tenants quickly is no proof that you're attracting the best tenants, which is what proactive landlords always want. Second, if you plan on owning multiple properties the combined effect of consistently charging below market rents will result in the loss of tens (or even hundreds depending how long you stay in the game and how many properties you own) of thousands of dollars over years.

I regularly see rents $150 below what I know the market will bear. It stuns me to imagine a landlord is willing to lose $1800 per year on a single property simply by not understanding the current market rents. If a landlord with 30 properties was as lazy as that they would lose $54,000 per year, which as you know, is the equivalent of a year's salary.

You may not have 30 properties yet, but it's a good idea to start thinking like a 30-property investor. These folks understand the power of accumulation of small things. Staying current on market rents is some of the most powerful knowledge you can have as you navigate your way through the filling vacancies process.

A New Starting Point

We've reached a milestone point in this book. Take a moment to look at everything learned until this point. Most, if not all, of reactive landlords don't execute everything you just learned as a matter of course. A truly reactive landlord will immediately jump into marketing for a new tenant attraction without completing all of the previous processes and systems.

They may do some of those components some of the time, but a reactive landlord doesn't have a consistent and repeatable system to do each of those things every time. Can you see why proactive landlords are so much more successful than reactive landlords?

It's no different than an NHL hockey player. When the average fan arrives at the arena to watch a game, we see highly trained and highly prepared athletes performing at a high level. What we don't see is the decades of preparation and practice that take place before they ever play their first game in the NHL. They don't just arrive at the arena the same day we do and start swiping at pucks.

Unfortunately, this is exactly the approach reactive landlords take. They don't understand that the preparation and following of proven processes is the path to being a successful landlord (and therefore real estate investor).

The Importance of Marketing

Proactive landlords understand the importance of landlording and execute accordingly. This is not necessarily an easy task considering the background many of us have. A lot of people get into real estate investing from a standard career where we just have one job to do that doesn't involve marketing.

For example, I was a teacher when I first started in real estate. Many others work in company offices. In fact, real estate investors come from pretty much every corner of the working world. This makes sense, as people are looking for security and wealth creation over the long term and real estate is one of the best vehicles to achieve this. However, if you don't have an entrepreneurial background (or even if you do) it can be very difficult to understand and apply the principles of marketing.

When I moved into real estate I didn't understand marketing, and it took me a while to get this component right. I don't know where you are personally on your real estate investing path, but I can promise you, if you don't already understand the importance of marketing in real estate, you soon will.

Just as every other aspect of filling vacancies (and landlording as a whole) this component must be systematized and carried out efficiently. Still, marketing requires a bit of creativity. It's not simply the application of a system, although a system is part of it.

Your Unique Selling Proposition

If you've never done any marketing you might be surprised to find out that the most important part of marketing is to first clearly understand your product (in this case, the property you are trying to rent).

No, it's not about hiring a graphic designer or an ad copywriter. The first task is to get crystal clear on your property's *unique selling proposition*. Whether it's the property's proximity to great schools, unique features, or proximity to major highways, your property must have some aspect that makes it different and therefore attractive to different kinds of tenants.

A property on a quiet cul-de-sac with old trees will be highly attractive to families, and a modern condo will be attractive to young couples or downtown yuppies. This might seem obvious, but knowing your ideal renter is the first thing you must do in order to understand your unique selling proposition. Knowing what makes the property unique mostly means knowing what makes it attractive to a certain kind of renter. Trying to market to the wrong person is bad marketing.

In my case, I buy and rent mostly single-family homes, townhomes, and duplexes. These products are perfect for families to live in. I invest in these kinds of properties because I prefer to rent to families, but this doesn't mean there aren't other great kinds of renters. I like families because I find they stay longer, and I prefer to minimize the vacancy filling process wherever possible, as it's the most time consuming phase (after the acquisition is complete). So for me, I'm clear that my renters are families that appreciate quiet neighbourhoods and proximity to schools and amenities. You will have to understand your ideal client and unique selling proposition before making the next step of marketing.

Jumping into design or copywriting before having clarity on the renter (and therefore the unique selling proposition) will result in a waste of time and money. Like most systems, marketing is actually quite simple. What's important is clarity and following the steps of the system to achieve maximal results, and the first step of that system, is to know the unique selling proposition.

The 3 P's of Marketing

When marketing, we must always focus on the 3 P's – Product, Price, and Promotion. With rental real estate **your** *product* **is the property. As discussed above, the key is to know your product's advantages and who you want living in it. This is the guideline one must use for writing marketing material.**

The second P is *price*. How are you going to be able to price your property to attract a particular tenant profile? This is dependent on the product, which will define the rent. Here it comes back to knowing your market as discussed above.

However, you must also consider the *seasonal market*. Due to our extreme Canadian weather, the rental markets are very sensitive to the time of year. Most Canadians don't move anywhere during winter, so if you're trying to rent a property in the cold winter months there is every possibility it will be harder to find tenants than during the other seasons – especially the busy spring months.

Unfortunately, if you're unlucky enough to have a property come up for rent at that time you may need to adjust the rent price down. The upside of this is that you can plan your leases to end during a better time of year to minimize the chances of having to deal with a vacancy at this time. By doing this you can increase the odds of having top-of-market (or near top) rents, which of course maximizes your ROI.

Other than the seasonal market issue, another factor for choosing price might be to have a *prompt payment discount*. This is a way you can use to attract tenants. Some tenants like the idea of paying less rent just by paying on time, so you can advertise the rent as one price with a discount for paying on time. Now, this may seem ridiculous. I mean, who would want to incentivize a tenant just for living up to their basic responsibilities? This seems like a bad management technique.

If it were a matter of losing rental income it would be a bad management technique. However, in reality you will just raise the basic rent to an above market price and when the tenant pays on time they will simply be paying the proper market rent. In essence a late rental payment at the higher rate would be a penalty, but the tenant would think it's the normal rent.

Understood this way, it might seem like the most intelligent way to price a property. Some landlords love it, but I don't usually use this system because I just haven't found that I really needed it. I carefully find, filter, and choose my tenants, so getting tenants to pay rent on time hasn't been a big problem. However, some landlords love this method because on paper it appears they are achieving a higher rent than they actually are receiving, which is helpful for financing future properties.

Rather than a prompt payment discount, I prefer to set a special maintenance agreement with tenants. Here the rent is set to full market price in the lease, but it's stated that the tenant will receive pay for maintaining the property. Then, when rent time comes, they simply pay the full rent minus the maintenance payment. I prefer this because it rewards special behaviour rather than just rewarding what's expected.

Make sure if you do this that you stipulate the minimum requirements outlined by your local bylaws. Yes, snow removal and yard maintenance are legislated in most jurisdictions. Setting these minimum standards with you tenants is an excellent strategy. It takes the onus off of you as the bad guy enforcing strict standards and puts it on your local jurisdiction. Setting this standard also gives you a guideline and legal grounds if the tenant regularly misses the bylaw enforced standard. If they fail to meet their obligation, you simply cancel the agreement with the tenant and hire a yard care company with the money you were paying the tenant. As with all the other documents mentioned in this book, you can find a sample of this agreement on my website at www.theontariolandlordtoolbox.com.

Going back to the prompt payment discount for a moment, remember that the amount you're allowed to offer for a discount is stipulated in the Residential Tenancies Act how much of an incentive you can legally offer. Know and understand this section of the Act before you do it. The Act states that "a discount in rent at the beginning of, or during, a tenancy of up to 2 per cent of the rent that could otherwise be lawfully charged for a rental period." Remember also that this would work better for more of a blue-collar tenant profile.

The last P is *promotion*. Here, I recommend keeping yourself open to any form of promotion available to you. When I say 'keep yourself open' I don't mean you should actually use every possible channel. This will exhaust you and lead to being overwhelmed. What I mean is to evaluate and consider all options, then focus effort on the channels that work best.

For example, I never use newspaper ads, but there might be geographic regions where this is the best method of promotion. I would be open to utilizing this (or any) method of promotion in the right circumstance. This is what I mean. Just keep yourself open to what will work for your specific market and tenant type.

Choosing which types of promotion to use will mostly come down to the particular type of tenant you have in mind. To find the right tenant you need to promote in the right places. Ask yourself what type of promotion your ideal tenant would be looking at. It's good to consider any and all avenues possible to promote your product, but depending on your model tenant and your property's market, not all avenues of promotion are equal. Still, it's a great idea to promote in any way possible.

Marketing to Existing Tenants – One of my favourite lines of promotion is through *existing tenants*. Proactive landlords utilize this line of promotion because we know that often the best tenants are found through existing great tenants. Great people usually have great friends, so a referral from a great tenant often works out well.

I maintain an email list for tenants, and regularly offer referral fees for any of my existing tenants who send me a new tenant. This works very well, and I often find excellent new tenants this way. One warning – if you really dislike a tenant make sure not to offer them the referral fee. Deadbeat tenants refer deadbeat friends, so it's best to stay away from that.

Neighbours – If you have a vacancy coming up you could let a few good neighbours know that you are looking for a new tenant. They might have a friend or family member that is interested in moving into the neighbourhood. The key here is to have an approach that helps your neighbours to understand that their friends and family are applying for a tenancy and it is not guaranteed.

Online Advertisements – Other than existing tenant referrals and neighbours the best way to usually find great tenants is through *online advertisements*. If you are wondering which web sites to use in your area, pretend you are a tenant and do a search on Google. If you have a basement apartment for rent in Pickering, you could do a search "Basement Apartment Rent Pickering" or "Apartment Rent Pickering" or "Basement Rent Pickering." See which web sites are the first 3 or 4 that come up, and advertise on those web sites. Those are the same ones that your tenants will use too.

I usually appeal to an online savvy kind of tenant, thus online advertising is a good strategy for me. Right now in my local area Kijiji is king. This is the number 1 place to advertise and find properties for rent. Unfortunately, Kijiji has lately begun charging users who rely heavily on their website. I know real estate investors who pay up to $750 per month to advertise on the Kijiji site.

Please note that this only becomes a problem when you have a certain amount of properties. Kijiji still allows a small number of ads per account, so if you only have up to 3 vacancies at a time you will not be charged.

Other than Kijiji, there is *Craigslist* and a number of other online advertising sites, including *Facebook* ads. They are all worth exploring. *Craigslist* (which is free) in particular attracts attention from people moving to the area from elsewhere. Kijiji is most popular in Ontario, but British Columbia and the entire U.S.A. uses *Craigslist*. I've never personally used *Facebook* ads, but I know other landlords who find them very effective. *Viewit.ca, Rentboard.ca* and *Gottarent.com* are paid sites also worth exploring.

The final thing worth mentioning about online ads is the security concern associated. Scammers will replicate your exact ad and ask potential tenants to pay them fraudulent deposits. As long as you're running a web ad, it's a good idea to scan for ads that look like your own and report them immediately to the website where you find them.

Newspaper Advertisements – I have never personally used *newspaper ads,* but this doesn't mean they're not a good idea for your market. In particular, I have heard from fellow investors that newspaper ads still work very well in smaller towns. I find the cost isn't worth the exposure compared to online advertisements in my market. In fact, having your advertisements online is a good early filter. You might want to ask yourself if you really want a tenant that doesn't know how to find a property for rent online. Again, this rule may not apply for your market such as small towns.

MLS – It's not too common in my region, but it may be a good idea to use the *MLS* to fill vacancies. The realtor fees are usually too high to justify this avenue, but it may be the best route to go when advertising a very high-end condo rental in downtown Toronto, for example. The key here is to know your own market. I don't use this method, which means I can't recommend it for middle class single-family homes, townhomes or smaller plexes in the Durham region. Here, I simply want to alert you to every possibility for promotion. Know your property type and market, and any type of promotion can work.

Supermarket Fliers – *Supermarket fliers* might work well for some neighbourhoods. A general rule of thumb is that most tenants for a neighbourhood will be found already living in that neighbourhood, so it makes sense to reach them directly through local sources.

Community Facebook Groups – Some communities have their own *Facebook groups*. If the community you invest in has such a group, then you will be wise to advertise your rentals there. This has the same effect as advertising in the local supermarket or other local mediums. It's a direct line to the small group of people already focused on your target community.

Facebook also has various public buy and sell and classifieds groups for different areas where you could post a vacancy. For example, the "Oshawa/Whitby Buy & Sell Group" has over 9300 members. Once you are in the group you can post your rental ad, which could then be liked and shared within *Facebook*.

Signs – Finally, there are good old-fashioned *window and lawn signs*. As with supermarket fliers and local *Facebook* groups, this targets people who are already in the local neighbourhood, and as you'll find from landlords everywhere it's often the single greatest source of tenant leads of any. This simple promotion is time tested and it works because the people already in the neighbourhood are the ones most likely to be looking for properties in the neighbourhood. Never overlook this simple form of promotion.

The main thing to remember about window and lawn signs is to follow the local bylaws. When holding an open house you can usually use directional signs that point to the property. These signs aren't typically allowed by bylaw to be left up full time, but for a weekend while holding an open house, it's usually allowed. Get yourself familiar with your local bylaws and use the maximum amount of local signage allowed.

Message (Ad Development)

Finally, once you've taken care of the product, the price, and have decided on the channels of promotion you're going to use, you can actually start writing your ads.

Luckily, you'll be mostly ready for this phase when it comes because writing ads is about knowing exactly who your customers are, what they want, and where they want to live. The property you offer for rent will be uniquely suited for your target client.

This specialization (when translated into marketing) is what we call the USP (Unique Selling Proposition) and it's based on the customers' needs, which informs the property you buy in the first place.

As you can see, all the activities you undertake as a landlord are connected. There is no sense marketing to families if you're buying properties for urban singles. This might sound painfully obvious, but I've seen landlords miss the mark in this way before. Marketing of a rental property and acquisitions are connected.

Having your USP helps demystify the process of writing ads, which is great because this topic can sound a lot more daunting than it actually is. You don't need a specialist education in advertising to figure this out – just let yourself be guided again by your customer's needs and your property's USP.

An ad must convey what the property offers, and you (the ad writer) must remember that below it all, a property offers a feeling or an emotion for the customer. Yes, if they have a family they need to know that the property is near schools and shopping, but they also need to know that it's on a quiet tree-lined street where they can rest assured their children will be able to play happily and safely.

To truly stand out, your ad must stir up emotion in the reader. This is known as the features vs. benefits distinction. Features are great for logically understanding what a property has to offer, but benefits paint a picture for us about how we'll feel in the property. This is important as emotions cause tenants to act. As a point of reference, take a look at this list of features:

- 3 bedrooms
- 2 bathrooms
- New appliances
- Close to shopping

Don't get me wrong. These are important to include in your ad copy. An ad is also a clear communication of the features of a property. It's great to stir up emotion in a potential customer, but if you don't also tell them exactly what's in the property you'll end up sorting through a lot of suspects. People can be emotionally drawn to your property through good ad copy, but you must ensure the ad clearly states what is and what isn't included in the property so that only tenants who would be a good fit will call.

In other words, to write effective ad copy you must include features, but benefits will really sell the property. Compare the following list of benefits with the above list of features:

- Plenty of Space for Kids to Play in this Massive Backyard
- Host the Best Summer BBQs in Your Private Yard
- Bask in the Warmth of South Facing Windows
- Entertain With Pride in Your Newly Renovated Home

Benefits paint a picture for us. If I'm a parent, looking to rent a house, I will be excited to know that the property I'm about to look at has a nicely sized backyard for my kids. It's the kind of emotion that makes me forget the price of a property and move to get it. On the other hand, "3 bedroom" does nothing for me emotionally. If I have 2 kids, then a 3 bedroom house is a necessity, so even if you hook me by describing a beautiful backyard, I won't call you unless you have 3 bedrooms. Highlighting features serves a practical function.

Put another way, there are a lot of 3 bedroom properties, but without good ad copy that paints an emotional picture for me about my kids' happiness, I wouldn't be drawn to any specific 3 bedroom property over another.

When developing ads, always ask yourself what sets your property apart from the competition? Knowing this, in conjunction with knowing exactly who your target tenant is and what they want, will allow you to focus on the benefits. But there is one more step. Ask yourself also what emotions and feelings your target tenants like to feel in a home. Is it:

- Coziness?
- Unity?
- Happiness?
- Pride?
- Togetherness?
- Being Elite?
- Intelligence?
- Privacy?
- Safe?

This is just a small list. There are no limits to the types of emotions tenants might feel in a particular property. For example, a university professor wanting to live next to the university he or she works at might want to be feel part of the educated community of the university neighbourhood.

My target tenants are families, so I always emphasize the emotions of safety, coziness, and togetherness that families seek. As an ad writer, it's your job to consider what your niche tenant is seeking and what your property has to offer.

Thinking Ahead

In this chapter, you just learned a simple system for attracting excellent tenants. As you saw, the marketing of your property goes hand in hand with the earlier (and concurrent) phases of the vacancy filling process.

If you understand your product well, have priced it right, and have promoted it well, you will have a steady stream of interested tenants. If you have a flood of interested tenants it might mean you're underpriced, a trickle might mean you're overpriced or haven't advertised to the right tenant profile of the neighbourhood.

No matter what the interest level, your attention must turn to what I call the "filtration system". Remember that the goal of real estate investment is to make money. This requires that you have excellent tenants. Sure, any landlord might get the odd dud of a tenant, but the proactive landlords that I know (myself included) rarely get duds.

The secret to bringing in an excellent tenant rather than a dud can be found in the filtration system you use. Not coincidentally, this is exactly the topic of the next chapter. Read the next chapter to find out how to separate the suspects from the prospects.

Try to be a filter,

not a sponge.

– STEPHEN CHBOSKY

CHAPTER 4

FILTRATION SYSTEM

Who Do I Want Living in My Property?

Have you ever seen a deadbeat tenant in the flesh? Worst yet, have you ever had a deadbeat tenant in a property of your own? If so, did you know in advance it was going to be a deadbeat tenant? Of course you didn't. If you knew, you wouldn't have let them move in.

Landlords let deadbeats move in every day, but nobody means to. It makes you wonder how it happens. Aren't there warning signs? Not many deadbeat tenants go around with a big sign on their chest that says, "Crazy". If they did, our job would be easier.

Instead, as proactive landlords we have to weed out the bad apples ourselves. The truth is that there *are* warning signs, but to detect them you have to follow the right process. The warning signs come out through the systematic steps of the filtration system, which we'll learn in this chapter.

We discussed marketing in the last chapter. Well-placed and well-written marketing material will bring a consistent stream of potential tenants to your door. That's great, but it's useless if you just go ahead and put the wrong tenant in the property. 'Useless' might seem like a strong word, but *you would be better off having a month of vacancy than putting a deadbeat tenant into the property.* A deadbeat will cost you far more than one month of vacancy.

So, up until now you have a carefully chosen property. It is renovated, prepped, and purposely suited to attract a certain type of tenant. It's also been smartly marketed using well-chosen resources. You should have leads by now, so the next crucial step is choosing which tenant is the best fit for this property and your investing system.

Now, how do you figure out which tenant is the right choice? How do you, not only narrow it down to the best applicant, but also sort through the people that are interested? There is much to consider? Fortunately, there is a process to ensure you won't get stuck with a dud. All you have to do is apply what I call a 'Filtration System.'

The Filtration System

Your first reaction, upon seeing 'filtration system' might be, "Oh great, more renovations. Sounds expensive." No, I'm not talking about an expensive water or air filter.

This is a no-renos-required filtration system. This filtration system is a streamline way to filter out the tenants you don't want, and then leave you with the best tenant options to choose from. To understand what I mean, let's go back to the original purpose of excellent landlording.

We invest in real estate to make money, which means having zero (or as close to zero as possible) vacancy. It's vital to have our properties full, but unfortunately this leads a lot of landlords to put just about anybody in their properties.

The problem with putting just about anyone in a property is that you are far more likely to end up with poor results. What do I mean by poor results? Well, how would you like a tenant that stops paying rent? This unfortunate situation almost always costs landlords money, even if we learn how to mitigate the risk of it well (to learn how read *The Property Management Toolbox: A How to Guide for Ontario Real Estate Investors and Landlords*).

Or worse yet, what about putting a truly degenerate tenant into one of your properties that not only stops paying rent but also causes purposeful damage to your property? Even if, as a proactive landlord, you seek restitution through legal means, the landlord almost always loses in this scenario.

Now, I can't 100% guarantee that you'll never experience one of these situations, but the risk of them can be greatly minimized by implementing a thorough filtration system. You would be absolutely shocked at how few landlords actually do this.

For example, in all of my time as a landlord I've never received a call from a new landlord doing a reference check on a former tenant of mine. To put that in perspective, I've dealt with at least 100 move-outs. That means of the 100 (or more) of my tenants who have moved out of my properties and into a new home, not a single landlord has called me asking how their new tenant was. As you'll see in this is one of the big components of the filtration system you'll learn here.

I *always* ask my incoming tenants for former landlord references, and I *always* call. Yet, I've seldom received a similar call. I've always thought this fact illustrates well how few landlords use a filtration system. On a broader scale, it illustrates how few landlords are proactive.

There are two key aspects you need to understand about this filtration system. First, as the name 'filtration system' indicates this is a *systematized* process with important steps that need to be followed in sequence to ensure incoming tenants are vetted thoroughly and efficiently. From when you pick up the first phone call inquiry about the property, to asking applicants the right questions at the right times, and to finally going to secondary sources and asking for referrals, this is a must-follow system.

Second, the filtration system prioritizes three landlording components. By following the filtration system you will focus on what's important. Namely:

- Your time – Nothing is more valuable, and the steps of the filtration system will allow you to get the most out of this prized commodity.

- Your property – the right tenant will treat and maintain your property in a way that keeps you informed about what is happening with it so you can make necessary repairs and so that unnecessary damages don't occur.
- Your tenant – The business and personal relationships you cultivate with your tenant will either cost you time and cause stress, or it will bring you profit and comfort. By using the filtration system correctly you will ensure a positive result.

Follow along with the steps, levels, and phases of the filtration system described below and you'll find that. Rather than hoping you've found the right tenant, you will have good reason to believe the wrong tenants have been eliminated and only the cream of the tenant crop will ever move in.

Fielding Calls

Just as when filtering water, your filtration system has various levels of filtration. The sooner you can filter the less than desirable suspects out of the funnel, the less time and effort they will cost you. If you can eliminate these suspects without ever speaking to them, it saves time and effort. Taking another step back, you can even look at your marketing efforts as the first level of filtration. By writing specific ads to attract only the tenant types that suite your property, not only will you attract the right tenants, but also seamlessly repel those who wouldn't be a good fit. What good is a system unless it saves you time?

Beyond marketing to tenants, though, into the actual filtration system, we can start this process by deciding how you choose to have tenants contact you. There are a couple of different ways to start this process and navigate your way through the potential tenants.

Proactive landlords seek to automate wherever possible. When setting up a system to field calls from prospective tenants is just such an opportunity. I use an online voicemail system run through www.*Grasshopper. com* – a web based multi-line phone system – to automate my tenant prospect incoming call process. Grasshopper allows real estate investors (or anyone) to systematize incoming phone traffic by setting up a series of toll free numbers. Other similar services are available like www. CanadaOneVoice.com and www.eVoice.com, but I prefer Grasshopper because of its ease of use.

This comes in handy when filling vacancies. I use a different number for each property in my ads. That way, when an interested tenant calls the number linked with the property they're interested in, they will hear a voicemail message that you create and explains the necessary details of the specific property they are interested in.

Once the recording ends, the caller will be prompted to leave a message with their contact info and any questions they might have about that property. This system allows the tenant to hear more about the property and make a decision about whether or not they want to continue pursuing the property before leaving a voicemail.

I always mention in the message that *verification* will be necessary for all tenants. Verification meaning that credit and reference checks will be done on every tenant that applies to rent a property. This deters some suspects, but moreover it informs and helps prepare the renter that verification will be a step in the renting process. (There will be more on verification in Chapter 6.)

This voice message system works well when fielding a large volume of calls as most landlords can't manage to pick-up every phone call and follow every lead as soon as it comes in – especially when you have a few vacancies at a time and/or have a full time job.

Instead, I set aside a dedicated time each day to sit down and listen to all the messages I've received, and with Grasshopper, I know what each message pertains to before I even listen to it, which helps with efficiency and time-management.

A system like Grasshopper isn't imperative for landlords with only a couple of properties – although it's highly recommended. What is imperative – regardless of portfolio size – is time management when fielding calls. The rule is batch efforts so you aren't wasting time. For standard tenant issues, such as property maintenance, I use separate phone extensions and usually listen to messages and respond within a day. For vacancies, it makes sense to check messages more often because the vacancy filling process is quick and dynamic. You don't want the best tenant to get away because you weren't quick enough on callbacks.

Regardless of how many properties you have, time is the most valuable commodity as you figure out how to get the most from your properties and grow your business.

Using Grasshopper to Track Ad Success

Grasshopper is wonderful for systemizing the tenant call-fielding process. However, you can take it even further by using it as a free testing service.

Whenever I'm trying to fill a vacancy for a new property type, tenant type, or new neighbourhood, I will set up a different Grasshopper line, not just for each property but also for each individual ad source.

This means there will be one line for Kijiji ads, another line for supermarket fliers, another line for community Facebook groups, etc. As normal, I check my messages regularly and simply keep a tally of the interest each ad source is generating.

This is particularly useful if you decide to pay for advertisement, as it gives you an opportunity to know for sure whether or not the cost is worth it. Even if you're not paying for it, tracking the success of each lead source will at least allow you to focus your advertising efforts where you get best results. This also prepares you for the next time you have a vacancy and to quickly determine the best method to promote your property and attract your ideal tenant.

Systemization always wins in landlording. Why place ads all over the place if one or two ad sources are bringing all the leads?

Tenant Questions

Once you've received a bunch of calls on your Grasshopper system or normal voicemail, you then have to speak directly to prospective tenants. Set aside one or two times per day to listen to all of the voicemails. Respond to each tenant to verify viewing times (this also must be batched for efficiency) to meet you and the property.

Once you're on the phone with an interested tenant is when you will get your first impression of them. Now is a chance to make sure you ask the right questions and that you aren't left wondering later about something you may have missed or forgotten.

To execute this, create a form with tenant questions for everything you need to ask of the tenant in that first conversation (go to www.theontariolandlordtoolbox.com to see a sample tenant phone questionnaire). If a tenant passes this initial telephone interview you can either move ahead with a viewing or move on to another tenant.

The list of questions and requests you need to ask are nothing out of ordinary but they are all essential. The form I use starts with their name, and then I ask them if they have a pen and paper. From there, I just start asking them a variety of questions to get an idea of who they are and where they are coming from. Things like:

- Where did you hear about our place for rent?
- How long do you want to rent for?
- How long have you been living at your current home?
- What pets do you have?

- How many people will be renting the place?
- Have you given your current landlord proper notice?
- What do you do for work?
- Do you foresee any problems paying the first and last month's rent?

After asking these questions, you move onto setting up a viewing. But first I'd like to offer a warning. There will be the odd case where you ask the tenant these interview questions over the phone and aren't satisfied with their answers – or their lack of straightforward answers. You may not want to show them the property based on what you hear.

If you do this, make sure to be careful about *how* you explain that you can't book a showing. You're better off to tell them you have another tenant already lined-up, so you're going in another direction rather than indicating it was anything they said that led you to go another direction.

Be conscientious about exact wording. On your interview sheet, write down some specific statements like "I have decided to go with another tenant" to help keep you on track when turning away a potential renter that does not seem to meet your renting criteria. There are human rights laws that could lead to problems if the tenant thinks they have been discriminated against and unfairly dismissed from being considered to rent the property. Don't be specific. Keep your words businesslike when a renter doesn't seem like the right fit. Never mention that you aren't choosing them because of a perceived fault of theirs.

Even if you aren't discriminating on the basis of gender, ethnicity, or any other unique situation (and you never should), it is easy to appear as though you are discriminating should there ever be a human rights tribunal – especially if you made a point of telling the prospective tenant that you were choosing not to put them in the property for a personal failing.

Book an Appointment to View

Once you have finished with the questions on your tenant phone questionnaire and are satisfied with the answers, invite the tenant to visit the property. Set a time and date, and make sure to be clear on the specifics like address and time. Make sure you tell someone when you are meeting a tenant – you never know what lurks on the other side of the phone. Ensure you are safe at all times by choosing times during the day or early evening when neighbours are home in case of anything going awry. This will save time giving directions later and will give you an indication of how well your potential tenants follow directions and listen.

Also request that they please call if they need to cancel. This request helps to hold them accountable. I even take this one step further by asking that the tenant give me a confirmation phone call no later than one hour before the scheduled showing. So, if we are supposed to meet at 7pm and they haven't phoned me by 6pm to confirm that they will be present for the viewing, then I assume that they have decided to not come and I won't show-up at the property as originally planned. This is another way to systematize your business, and there are two reasons for this little system.

First, tenants often don't show-up for a showing because they may have found another property. Rather than cancel, they just do a no-show. If they are serious, though, and if they want to see the property, they will confirm with a call. When they do, you will know you still have to be there for the viewing. If the confirmation call doesn't come in, then you can move ahead with your schedule and won't end up wasting time by attending a meeting where the other party does not show up. Again, time is your most valuable commodity.

Second, the confirmation call sets a precedent for the numerous deadlines and schedules the potential tenant will need to meet and uphold. For example, they will have to provide necessary information and documentation for the application process, making rent payments, and eventually submitting a vacancy notice properly. The sooner they understand the nature of your relationship (accountability and expectations) the smoother things will run for both of you.

The Power of Relationships

We've spoken of relationships a lot in this book. Relationships are the single most valuable asset you have in this business. This can't be overstated. Having excellent relationships makes money for proactive landlords every day. On the other hand, reactive landlords lose money every day by not cultivating excellent relationships.

Take for example one situation I had with a tenant, Jason (not his real name), who'd given me notice to vacate after only having lived in the property for 6 months even though he was under a 1-year lease. Now, I could have taken the hard line approach and told the tenant that he was obliged to stick out the lease or else there would be a big penalty. In fact, in this situation the tenant even gave me short notice. Not only did he not finish his lease, but he also wanted out within 30 days.

I could have easily told him it wasn't possible and that he was on the hook for the extra month of rent. In such a case, we have to ask ourselves, "Who is going to win from such an attitude?" The reality is that nobody wins, least of all the landlord. So, why do something that doesn't benefit you or the tenant? The relationship is more important, and I made a decision for the relationship.

Still, I had to protect myself, so I had an honest face-to-face conversation with the outgoing tenant about his responsibilities and what I'd do. I explained that I'd do everything in my power to get the property rented out in time for him to meet the move-out deadline he was seeking.

I informed Jason that if I couldn't find a new tenant for the month after his move out date that he would be on the hook for rent, but that I'd do everything I could. I also asked him to help me however he possibly could, especially by being helpful with showings.

Jason kept the property spotless and made sure that showings went smoothly. We worked together, and in the end we were able to find a tenant in that short amount of time. The outgoing tenant even paid for my advertising costs, as we had a clear understanding of responsibilities.

It was a bit of work, but by committing to the relationship, the best possible outcome happened. The new tenants were excellent, so I was happy. In fact, I was thrilled as the new tenants ended up staying two years and were excellent. Jason was so happy that he referred me to one of his friends, who eventually became an excellent renter in one of my other properties.

The moral of the story is that you always win by being committed to the relationship. It's not always a straight line from your effort success, but relationship always wins. Think about how different things might have been if I would have taken the confrontational approach and demanded he stay to the end of his lease.

You don't want to keep someone in your property that doesn't want to be there, and all it takes to avoid this problem is to work for the relationship. It's called being solution oriented, and it's the way you have to approach every landlording situation.

Pre-Application Process

By this point, you have put the tenant through two filters in your filtration system. The first filter was the voicemail system. The second filter was you calling them back to ask some basic questions and get your first impression of them. The third filter is what I call the pre-application process.

This takes place at the viewing and is of utmost importance. It's an important level in the filtration process but is less obvious and straightforward than the first two levels. This filter will require you to make decisions using your gut instinct, or your natural detective skills, or your BS detector – whatever it is you use to decide if a person is honest, genuine and reliable. It's a fairly simple process to understand but that doesn't mean it's necessarily easy to execute.

The method is to ask the tenant questions while showing them around the property. Other than the questions you ask though, you want to talk very little while getting them to talk as much as possible. Focus on listening closely to what they're saying and how they're saying it. Your goal is to decide whether or not their story makes sense based on the following criteria:

- Why are they interested in this property?
- Is this property close to their work?
- Why do they want to move?
- Do they need more space?
- Is their decision to move a matter of proximity to work or their kids' schools?

- Is it for convenience reasons or financial reasons?
- Do they like the neighbourhood?
- What other properties have they looked at?
- Does their current landlord know they are looking at other properties?

Based on the prospect's answers to these questions, you then reflect to yourself. Be honest with yourself whether or not you like and accept the answers they are giving you. Do you like what they are telling you, or do you feel like they're only telling you want they think you want to hear?

This is really a gut instinct filter. Unlike most of the systems you will read about in this book, it's more of an art and will take practice. Then again, most relationship-based practices are art instead of science. This doesn't mean we can't get better at selecting excellent tenants.

With some experience, you will start to develop instincts and methods for how to extract the responses and conversational behavior that will help you decide if this person is a good prospective tenant or a dud.

Let me point out here that most people you come across won't be dishonest. Most are just looking for a place to live that suits them based on their needs, their resources, and their situation. But there are those select few – members of the notorious 3% -- that will try to deceive. It's imperative to identify these people using this pre-application level in your filtration system.

Eliminate Suspects

Based on what you find out from the walkthrough, questioning, and listening at the pre-application level you will then have to eliminate the suspects. So, what are some warning signs to be aware of? I am most leery about these symptoms:

- **Gaps in the story** – Where did they live or work for the six-month period between what they have told me about? Unless they were travelling, or working in a remote area, or something of that rare nature, then there shouldn't be more than a few weeks to a month (maximum) where they can't account for a place of residency or a job.

- **Tendency to changes jobs and residencies often** – Why is this happening? Is it their own choice or are they being forced out? Being the type of person that enjoys variety and change is one thing, but unreliability is a matter that a landlords need to beware of.

- **Vague motives for wanting to move** – If people want to move, the answer should be apparent and easily answerable. Most moving tenants want more space, to be closer to work, or have to change due to a recent change in relationship status. If they just say 'felt like a change' or 'no particular reason,' you might want to question further.

- **The biggest story** –I find the person with the biggest story may lead to the biggest troublemaker. When a person can't stop talking about how poorly they were treated by ex-landlords or about how things never seem to work out at jobs, then there is a good chance of trouble. This supposed string of 'bad luck' will not stop at the front door of your property. If you hear such a story, just keep in mind that the longest, most detailed, and overly dramatic story, is often more fiction than truth.

When any of these warning signs are easy to recognize or even moderately present, it's probably in your best interest to tell the tenant you still have a couple more viewings booked for the property. Tell them you will get back to them soon about the property's availability.

Call them the next day and explain you've decided to go in another direction, return to your lead generation system, and once again begin to explore other potential tenants.

Identify Prospects

It might sound like the majority of people that call are bad seeds worthy of your cynicism, but this isn't true. There are plenty of great tenants out there, and just as you need to identify the bad tenants, you also need to identify the good ones.

So, what are the signs of a reliable and honest prospect? It's usually quite straightforward, and if your properties are located in areas with low vacancy rates, then it won't be difficult to find and choose a good prospect. Their qualities aren't too difficult to determine. Mostly they are the *opposite of what the suspects* will show and tell you. Here are some positives to watch for:

- **Forthcoming and direct answers** – If they are excited and interested in the property, there will be no hesitance or vagueness in their words. They will be looking at the property as a potential home, telling you what they like and what they are looking for. They are excited about seeing their things in their new space.

- **They come prepared** – Prospects often come with documents, references, and ready to submit all anticipated information. However, don't mistake eagerness for an inclination to skip steps. There is a difference between willingness to cooperate and rushing to sign papers and grab keys. Never let a tenant rush you.

- **A plausible story** – "We just got new jobs and are moving to town," "It's closer to my work," "We need more space because our kids are getting older and this seems like a better neighbourhood for our family," are the kinds of responses that make sense and are easy to verify.

The people giving you these types of answers who are providing this kind cooperation and feedback are the ones you'll come to spot quickly. When you see an excellent prospect, it's time to move to the fourth level in the filtration process.

The Application

If you've come this far, it means the prospective tenant has already passed 3 levels of filtration. The closer the tenant moves to the end of the filtration system the more likely they are to be a good tenant. However, just as a water-filter catches finer and finer particles as the water moves nearer the end, so too does your filtration system catch smaller and smaller hints as you near the end of the process.

Once you've decided (after the phone interview and property-viewing/interview) that the prospect appears to be a worthy tenant and both parties are ready to move forward, then the next step is to have the tenant complete your *Application for Rental Accommodation* Form (see www.theontariolandlordtoolbox.com).

This should happen at the end of the viewing appointment. Some applicants will ask to take the application home, then will return it soon after, as they may not have all the necessary information on hand. This is fine, too.

However, it's generally better when the applicant completes the form with you present, as there is then less chance for them to be selective about the information they provide (more on this below). Plus, it has the added benefit of moving the process along quicker. It's better to have a great tenant make some kind of commitment wherever possible, whatever that commitment might be, as it creates a sense of obligation on their part toward you and your property.

It's important to note that the application for rental accommodation form is not the official lease or contract. This is still another layer of the filtration system to apply before having a prospect sign the lease.

The application outlines the terms of the lease, lays out precise features of the property, provides schedules and structures of important dates, and asks for some specific details about the tenant. This form is meant to make the tenant aware of what they will eventually be agreeing to when they sign the lease.

The form I use is broken into four sections over two pages.

The first section of the application for rental accommodation form includes:

- **Landlord and lease information**: name, address, contact info, the date that the proposed lease would begin, and the rate of the monthly rent.

- **Property details**: address, appliances, utility description and duties (snow removal, gardening, etc.)

- **Terms of deposit**: Applicant(s) will pay a deposit of $_____ to be used as a contract deposit only and shall be deemed a rent deposit upon occupancy.

The second section of the application for rental accommodation form includes:

- **Applicant(s) information**: name, address, phone, email, place of work, date of birth, driver's license number (car year and model), social insurance number, emergency contact info, bank info – also include a privacy clause.

- **Tenancy and employment history**: All addresses and places of work from last seven years, as well as contact info for landlords and employers.

- **Other Residents**: Names, ages, and relationship to the applicant of the people who will occupy the premises in addition to the applicant. Note: Spouses or Co-tenants must fill out a second separate application.

- **Miscellaneous**: Inquires about tenant's insurance, bankruptcy, pets, etc.

The third section of the application for rental accommodation form includes:

- **Privacy compliance**: States that the applicant(s) agree to apply to rent the residential premises as this form lays out.

- **Recognition**: Applicant administers their signature, writes the date, and checks off a box stating that they 'have read, understood and voluntarily agree to the terms and conditions, and the collection use and disclosure of information as outlined above.'

The fourth section of the application form is for your use or for the use of any clerical staff you may have. It includes places for you to record the date you received the application, a place to initial who received it, and confirmation of having seen picture ID of the applicant.

Process Application

Once the application form is complete and submitted, you can begin to process it with two important steps: calling current and former landlords and calling current and former employers. These are the latest steps in the filtration system, which if executed, will put you in a small percentage of proactive landlords.

Landlords Reference Checks

When you contact other landlords to confirm an applicant's current and previous residencies, you will have to once again put some trust in your gut instinct to determine if what you're hearing is the truth. This is because you can't necessarily trust what a tenant's current (outgoing) landlord says about the tenant

You might think this sounds a bit bizarre. I mean, why on earth would a previous landlord want to lie? To answer that question you have to consider the landlord's motivation. It's a unique circumstance since the prospect's current landlord may have her own priorities in mind rather the applicant's.

Let me explain.

Imagine your prospect is a model tenant. Then their current landlord may not want to lose that tenant, even if the tenant wants to move. So, you could be talking to a landlord about someone who has been a great tenant and the landlord might give that tenant a terrible reference because they don't want their model tenant to move.

In this case, the landlord is trying to sabotage the tenant as a prospect for other landlords. If this was the case, the worse the reference would mean a better the tenant. On the other side of this coin, seemingly great feedback could be a ploy by the outgoing landlord to get a bad tenant off their hands. They will want to improve the chances that you give an applicant a new place to live because the applicant is actually a horrible tenant. This might sound farfetched to some, but it has happened to me.

I'm not suggesting you don't call the prospect's most recent landlord. By all means call them and use your gut instinct to determine whether or not they're telling the truth or not. However, don't rely completely on instinct.

I always put a lot more stock in the referral of the 2nd most recent landlord. They have no attachment to the tenant at that point, so you can trust that they will tell you the truth more than the most recent/current tenant.

If both landlords corroborate the same account of your prospect, then you have good reason to believe the story. If there is disagreement between the two landlords' stories, I trust the 2nd most recent landlord every time.

When doing landlord reference checks, you're not just shooting from the hip. Just as when interviewing applicants, you must have questions ready when you call other landlords for reference checks.

I use a standard form for this, which can be found at www.theontariolandlordtoolbox.com. The line of questioning is straightforward. Explain why you're calling, who it's in regards to, confirm their name and the residency details, and then just start asking your fellow landlord the questions:

- How long have you known the tenant?
- In what capacity do you know them?
- How would you describe them?
- How do they get along with others?
- How did they keep the place?
- Did they have difficulty paying rent on time?
- Did you know he/she was looking at other residences?

You may have some follow-up questions to these, but this conversation should give you a pretty good idea about the tenant's previous living situation.

You might assume this is a bothersome practice for the landlord receiving the call, but remember they don't receive many of them. As mentioned above, I've rarely been contacted for a reference check on a former tenant.

I find this astonishing.

Reference checks are quick and easy. The phone numbers needed to execute them will be displayed on the application (hint: if the prospect didn't include references then they're a suspect) Once you have the numbers, just sit down with a pen and paper, dial the number and talk to the reference for a few minutes to get the critical information.

These reference checks are fast, simple and are an incredibly valuable filter.

It's the difference between filtering out a member of the 3% or not.

Think about it. What will a person who (semi-professionally) exploits people and burns all their bridges not have? Good references. They will be forced to lie and provide false information in order to fill out an application. This why you call references provided and utilize intuition.

In spite of how easy it is, most landlords just aren't doing reference checks – like I said, I've never done a single one for a previous tenant. Don't be a lazy landlord! Do reference checks!

Not Trusting Gut Instinct – The Makings of a New Policy

As a landlord, you will have to develop a strong gut instinct, but instinct alone isn't enough of a tool for making decisions. Listen, I talk about gut instinct in this book. I believe there is a place for gut instinct, especially in times when the process can't help you. There comes a point when you have all of the information, and then you just have to make a decision.

Sadly, there is no such thing as perfect risk reduction. There will always be some risk. When it comes to putting a tenant into one of your properties, there is always that chance that you'll end up with a dud.

I can handle the odd (very odd) dud of a tenant as long as I can look in the mirror after the fact and tell myself I did everything humanly possible to minimize the chance of it happening. If I completed every step of the system, then made judgment to the best of my ability with the information I had at the time, then I will be able to live with the consequences.

Often you don't have to rely on gut. The bad tenants often weed themselves out and the good ones find their way to you. There's not much gut instinct at play when all the factors make sense and each part of the story fits with the next.

However, you will find yourself in the odd situation where no amount of information will be enough to remove risk entirely, and then you have to rely on gut instinct. So, I believe instinct has a place, but there is a big warning here. When you receive evidence that explains a situation without having to use gut instinct, you must adjust.

Here's the point: if you get burned by not trusting your gut you must seek the lesson in the situation. Think about what specifically happened that caused the situation. Worse yet, you might actually trust your gut instinct, but then it ends up being wrong. Again, look for the lesson in the situation. What factor caused the problem?

There was a reason your instinct was muddled – whether right or wrong. So, after the fact, ask yourself what factor was different about the situation that caused you to make the wrong decision. What am I driving at here?

Allow me to explain.

I experienced a situation (before developing my system) where I didn't listen to my gut instinct, and I got burned badly. The good news is that I'm certain this will never happen to me again (in exactly the same way) because I used the negative experience to develop new policies and systems (for a thorough discussion of policies and how to develop new ones, please refer to *The Property Management Toolbox: A How to Guide for Ontario Real Estate Investors and Landlords*).

It happened when I put a single-family home up for rent using my normal marketing system – or at least what was my normal marketing system at the time. I've come a long way since then, and my marketing is much better. More importantly, I'm far more focused on the kinds of tenants I seek for my properties now. I know exactly what kinds of tenants are going to be living in my properties before I even put up an ad. This is important.

So, I put up some general marketing based on my lack of focus, and as a result, I got a mixed bag of tenant types interested. To be honest, the interest in the property wasn't that strong. I didn't want to have a vacancy, so I focused on a group of three young women who had applied and seemed very interested.

By the way, that statement – that I didn't want a vacancy, so I chose whoever was interested – marked the beginning of not following my gut instinct and my downfall on this property.

Now, as you know by now, I hate vacancies. I believe there are very few reasons to have vacancies. These days, with a better marketing system in place and more focus on my property and tenant type, I rarely get a vacancy. My average vacancy rate is well below the market average, where it should be and where yours should be when you implement this system. I hate vacancies, but the only thing worse than a month of vacancy is putting a bad tenant (or set of tenants) into a property. The bad tenants will cost you more than the month of vacancy by minimum double – every time. Moreover, they will cost you a lot of time and stress, which is even worse.

So, I zoned in on a group of three young women and went through the filtration process that I did have. One of the young women was a nurse, another was a first-year student (and the nurse's sister), and the third was another first-year student (the friend).

My gut instinct was saying no, but my mind came up with some clever justifications that told me to let the girls move-in. First, I told myself, "Well, the older sister is a nurse. She's a grown-up and she'll keep the others in check."

Wrong.

Think about the self-delusion of this story. First year university students are notoriously worse than high school students when it comes to responsibility. They are hurled out into the world, still never having dealt with real world consequences, and (often) have little regard for their own health let alone grown up concerns like rental properties. Parents notoriously have a hard time making sure their teenage kids stay out of trouble, and nobody is more invested than a parent. An older sister, who is barely out of university, doesn't stand a chance. Nevertheless, I took it as gospel truth that the older sister would 'make sure the others stayed in line'.

My second justification might have been even more flimsy. I thought to myself, "Well, the older sister is employed, so the younger sister and her friend probably have good parents who will make sure they always pay their rent and are responsible."

This is a big stretch. The older sister or the parents (imagined) responsibility no bearing on how the two first year students are going to behave. Had I never heard of a fine upstanding person whose son or daughter was wild and irresponsible in university? Of course I had, but on this occasion I let justification get in the way of the truth.

You see, there were good reasons that I was feeling a gut instinct against letting these girls move in. At the time I lacked the policy, the experience, the process, and the knowledge to filter out these suspects.

Nevertheless, the three girls moved in, and for the first little while, it appeared as though everything would work out just fine. The turning point came when the nurse emailed me a few months later to tell me that she was going to leave the property. Her wording was priceless. She said, "I can't take it anymore."

She told me the partying was relentless, that she had barely had an ounce of sleep in the past 3 months, and that she was sick of having to clean the house every single day just to get it to a minimally livable level, but that was just the tip of the iceberg.

She went on to tell me that the two university students had a friend who would invite herself over any time of the day or night. This "friend" wouldn't come alone, though. She brought men with her – different men each time. In fact, the nurse told me that the friend was running a prostitution ring out of the basement.

What?

The strangest thing about the whole 'affair' was that I had been in for an inspection not long before. I still had that gut instinct going on, so I conducted a property inspection three months after they moved in. They must have cleaned up well for my visit because everything appeared to be in order for the most part.

I noticed there was bed in the basement during that inspection, but I just assumed it was a spare for when friends stayed over. An extra bed in a basement is not out of the ordinary enough to make a judgment that something as bizarre as a prostitution ring was going on.

Nevertheless, this was exactly what happened.

There was just one little problem with the nurse wanting to get out. All *three* of the young women were on the lease. This meant that she was legally responsible for anything that might happen in the property. Deciding to leave because she couldn't take it anymore just wasn't a possibility – so much for her being the grown up and responsible one. She hadn't even properly understood the lease she signed.

In fact, this event was one that pushed me to develop a much more robust system for explaining responsibilities to each tenant, as it occurred to me that she hadn't taken the time to understand it, given her belief she could just cut and run.

I explained all of this in a strongly worded email, and I suggested that we just terminate the lease altogether, which would require my approval along with all three of the tenants. The nurse, after learning she couldn't run away from the problem, quickly agreed that a mutual termination of the lease was the best possible solution.

Unfortunately, the other two dug in their heels. Isn't that the way it always is? The two whose irresponsibility had led to the trouble in the first place were the least willing to amicably resolve the situation.

Eventually, I managed to set up a meeting at a local coffee shop with all 3 of the girls, myself, and a more experienced colleague of mine. I thought he could help us come up with a solution to the problem (i.e., talk some sense into the two students). The next that wanted to leave was the sister's friend. After explaining that the best thing to do for everyone was to mutually agree to terminate the lease, (after I found a new tenant), the sister's friend finally decided to leave.

I could imagine the conversations they were having together at that time. There were two who wanted out, and only one who wanted to stay. They knew after our coffee shop chat that for anyone else to move in I would have to approve them, since this was my right in the lease.

Under no circumstance was I willing to let anyone move in without first going through a rigorous filtration process – more rigorous than the first time. I would need income verification and solid references. Finally, under pressure from the other two, the last holdout relented, and they agreed to mutually terminate the lease after I found a new tenant to replace them.

Once I started showing the property, I discovered a bunch more reasons (beyond the partying and the prostitution ring) that overruling my gut instinct was a bad choice.

First, I discovered that the girls had three dogs that they were sneaking into and out of the property. They didn't have (or claimed they didn't have) the dogs when they moved in, and these were big slobbery dogs, too. Luckily, the dogs didn't cause too bad of damage, but I was mortified at the potential for damage caused by their deception. I wondered what else they might have deceived about.

This was the event that eventually helped me figure out that I needed a pet addendum on my lease. If you're counting, that's the second policy/system change that this experience forced upon me.

However, the biggest policy change was to never rent a property to students unless it is dedicated student housing. I have nothing against students. In fact, many landlords cultivate the student-housing niche with great success, but a student house isn't a family house, and never the two shall meet.

You might wonder what the difference is. Well, there is location for one, but the most important factor that separates a family rental from a student rental is that every tenant is a student, and every student must have their mom, dad, or both as guarantors. This means you qualify student tenants on the basis of their *parents' income*.

This qualification process accomplishes two things. First, since the parents are guarantors it means the students immediately become more responsible. They make better choices when they know they have to answer to mom and dad. Second, if they fall off the responsibility wagon, you're still covered by the parents (who you know have the cash based on the income verification process).

Never putting students in non-student housing became official policy for me after this event. I started with a gut instinct that something wasn't right. I didn't listen to that gut instinct and put myself in a costly and time-consuming situation as a result.

However, I used that failure of decision making as a reflective opportunity in order to grow my thinking, inform policy and process going forward. This is what I recommend for every landlord. Use decision-making failures to create successful new policy. To do this, simply look for the unique factors of the failure of decision and apply them in the future.

Employer Reference Checks

Calling current and former employers is just as vital as calling former landlords. There is nothing quite like knowing your prospect is not only gainfully employed, but moreover has a sterling record of service to put your mind at ease. Conversely, it feels great to catch a perpetual rogue by talking to current or former employers. This could save you a lot of hassle and money as nobody is less qualified to pay rent than someone without a steady income.

A warning: just as you must verify the truthfulness of the former landlord's words, you must also verify the employer. A critical level of due diligence in this is to find out whether or not the employer/company actually exists. Luckily, with the Internet it's not difficult to find out about a prospect's employer. To verify whether you've been given legitimate information, simply Google the name of the employer along with the phone number provided. If the phone number and name of the company don't appear to match there is a very good chance the prospect has given you a dummy phone number. When this happens, it's usually a friend or family member who will pose as an employer while giving the prospect/suspect a glowing review.

In one instance I had an applicant use his sister as a false reference. While his sister did hold a managerial position at a known company, the applicant was not an employee at the company. Once I figured out the applicant used his sister as a reference and didn't disclose their relationship, I moved the applicant into the suspect file.

I learned the truth by a simple Google search. There is a lot of information available online, so never hesitate to type an applicant's name, their place of work, their employer's name, or anything else that might come to mind into a search engine and see what useful information you can find.

Once you do call an employer for a reference check, the same line of questioning used with the landlord doubles easily. Only a few modifications are required. An added perk with questioning employers as opposed to landlords is an employer's motives should generally align with the applicant's, as most employers would want an employee to have a proper accommodation so as to not interfere with their ability to work and be an asset to their company.

Suspects Filtered Out

You just learned about a no renovations required filtration system that can and will save you enormous cost and time if you follow the process. In fact, following such a system is your best shot at getting a reliable and trustworthy tenant.

The most important thing to remember when implementing your filtration system is to plan your steps in the correct order and execute your tasks properly before you leave one step and move on to the next. Here's a breakdown:

1. **Taking calls from interested applicants** – Develop a disciplined and efficient system for fielding phone calls so you don't waste time and get interrupted by repetitive phone calls.

2. **Learn to interview applicants** – Whether it is on the phone or at the viewing make sure to get all the necessary information you require in order to make an informed and valid judgment about a potential tenant. (Practice with a spouse or friend to gage your responses, and 'gut reactions'.)

3. **Identify suspects and prospects** – Learn and memorize what the signs of a good tenant versus a bad tenant are so that while you're interacting with applicants it becomes second nature to identify the telling traits.

4. **Put your application to work** – Use the tenant application as a tool for determining if the tenant is honest and open when it comes to providing extensive personal information.

5. **Call references** – Use referral information from landlords and employers (that tenants put on the application). It's okay to trust prospective tenants, but it's not okay to be lazy. Pick-up the phone and call those references. It can be the difference between a good tenant and a deadbeat tenant.

Did you notice all it really takes is a telephone, some people skills, and a keen ear? Apply those simple tools and they will help you manage your time efficiently and assist in you in finding the best tenant for your property.

However, the filtration system is not yet complete. As I said, these are all the filters *to this point*. There is another crucial filter explained next, and without it, all the preceding filters are meaningless.

It's called a credit check, and it's another important step to the vacancy filling system. A friendly smiling face that gives you a good gut feeling are not enough to accept a new tenant. A credit check that is not in-line with the story that tenant has been telling you, can be an excellent tool saving you many hours of time and money on an eviction.

The next chapter contains imperative information on how to read and understand a credit report and how to protect you from becoming an entry on a bad credit report.

"*Too many people spend money they haven't earned, to buy things they don't want, to impress people that they don't like.*"

– WILL ROGERS

CHAPTER 5

CREDIT CHECK AND CONDITIONAL ACCEPTANCE

The Million-Dollar Question: Where's the Rent?

Doesn't it seem easier to make decisions when there is some form of external validation? This isn't always available to us as real estate investors. There are times, such as when seeking financing, that we have some form of external validation for our decisions, but it's not too regular. However, one of those moments is available after we complete our filtration system and move onto the credit check.

If you've come this far in the system it means you've met some potential tenants. Let's imagine they seem like nice people. They're friendly, kind, well mannered, and trustworthy. You've even done reference checks and received great feedback, so this must be the kind of tenant you want to do business with right?

Not so fast.

You haven't yet confirmed that the tenant can be counted on to fulfill their responsibilities when it comes to the most crucial part of the whole business – the part about paying rent.

If you had to pick between a sweetheart of a tenant that's late (or absent) with rent payments, or a jerk that makes sure every rent cheque is signed, sealed and delivered on the last day of the month, who would you pick? You don't have to answer that. I'm a landlord too, so I already know your response.

As a landlord, rent is all-important. You depend on rent. It's why you got into this business. So, if on the first of the month the rent cheque isn't there, you have a real problem. This is where the next filter comes into play: The Credit Check. Knowing a tenant's history of making payments in the past might be your best indicator of whether or not they will be a trustworthy rent payer.

You will get to examine a credit report and analyze concrete numbers, but before you do this, you need to understand what you're looking for. You need to know what you can sometimes let slide, what you can never let slide, and what the heck those R9s mean. In this chapter I'll explain:

- How to read and decipher what a credit report is telling you
- What information to place emphasis on

- What information to take with a grain of salt
- When to be understanding
- When to be savvy
- What Conditional Acceptance is and what it means for the tenant

Keep in mind, you don't have to be an accountant to complete a credit check and gather information. You just need two things. First, you need an interest in collecting on-time rent cheques. Second, you need to read and understand this chapter. You already have the interest in collecting rent cheques, so just read on to learn the rest.

Credit Checks

After putting the tenant through various filters and sifting through the evidence provided – sometimes relying on gut intuition, you now get to analyze some concrete numbers with a credit check. Feels good, doesn't it?

Always do the credit check after you've phoned and done reference checks. Credit checks cost money, which means it's a waste of money to do a credit check first only to find out afterwards from a previous landlord or employer that the applicant would make a horrible tenant.

Some tenants will bring their own credit report, which is fine and it doesn't hurt to take a look at it, but always do your own. Bringing their own credit report may just be a proactive step by an eager applicant, and the report they provide may be an official and up to date credit check.

However, it could also be a forged or manipulated report meant to make you believe that you can skip doing a credit check on your own. A reactive landlord (without a standardized system) may fall for this, but you're a proactive landlord, which means you must do your own credit check.

If you've never done one, please don't worry. It only *sounds* official and difficult. It's actually simple and seamless. The only preparation you have to make is ensure the prospect has signed a credit check consent form, which is part of their rental application (go to www. theontariolandlordtoolbox.com for a sample application form with credit check consent form).

Rent Check and R Ratings

Rent Check Credit Bureau is an efficient and reliable way to check an applicant's credit. You simply go to their website – www.rentcheckcorp.com – and use the applicant's legal name and social insurance number to generate their credit report. Members of various clubs and organizations will get a discount for using their services. There are other tenant screening services available to Canadians like www. tenantverification.com and www.backcheck.net.

Once you have the credit report in your hands, you're looking for "R ratings". It might not be as much of a thrill as seeing an illicit movie when you're too young, but it might spook you just as much depending on what you see.

Remember that everyone has "R ratings" on their credit report. It's the number that follows the R that's pertinent to landlords. That crucial number comes from credit-reporting agencies, such as banks or credit card companies, who have either past or present payment plans with an applicant. The credit-reporting agency assigns a number to the 'R', which is dependent on whether the applicant's payments were made on time, late, or not at all. The numbers assigned range from 0 to 9.

An R0 means that the item is too new, or has been approved and not used. R1 to me is the best rating, and it means that on that particular account (a car loan for example) payments were made within 30 days of the payment due date. So, if an applicant had a car loan that lasted three years and paid every payment in that three-year period on-time except for one, then they would get an R1 rating from that agency.

An R9 rating is the worst. If you see this it means the applicant has either been deemed as having bad debt that's been placed for collection, or has claimed bankruptcy and moved without giving a new address.

If an applicant simply quit making payments, and the credit-reporting agency placed their balance in collection, then they would get an R9 rating. Or, if the applicant filed for bankruptcy, and didn't report that they were moving, they would get an R9 rating.

Getting a rating between 0 and 9 depends on how long a person has gone without making a payment. For instance, having a payment over 30 days late will lead to an R2 rating, having a payment that is over 60 days late will be an R3 rating, and so on.

Using this rating system, it seems like an applicant with R1 ratings would mean an easy approval is in order, and that an applicant with an R9 rating would be a simple decline. In some cases, this would be so. I would say that, while R1 ratings are easy to base a decision upon, there is more to consider with an R9, before coming to a definite conclusion.

Story of the Credit Check

A credit check reads much like a story, complete with a timeline, settings, and key plot points. It's your job to see if the credit check story agrees with the rest of the story the applicant has told. They've told you where they've lived and worked, and you will have verified those stories with references. Altogether, your questions and conversations (with the prospect and his/her references) have created a character description for you. The credit check story simply corroborates the story from the prospect.

Unless there has been an error in the credit reporting (which does happen) the credit check doesn't lie. There may be some missing information that needs to be filled-in, but the point of the credit report is that it reports directly on the facts. The applicant (on the other hand) could have lied. Assuming there have been no errors on the credit report, it's a perfect chance to find out if the prospect has been honest with all the information provided.

For instance, on the *Application for Rental Accommodation* the applicant would have answered 'yes' or 'no' to whether or not they've ever filed for bankruptcy. The credit report will tell you this fact. If they've answered 'no' on their application but the report says 'yes', then you have a major warning sign. Bankruptcy itself might not be a deal breaker, but lying about bankruptcy is a bad sign.

If they answer 'yes' to bankruptcy it shows a lot of courage. Nobody wants to be exposed for a difficult financial past. An honest 'yes' is not necessarily a deal breaker. I have put tenants in my property that have been bankrupt in the past, and I would do it again. Let me explain.

When to be Understanding

People sometimes get divorced, which can get messy and expensive. People sometimes lose jobs through no fault of their own. People sometimes suffer health problems that are out of their control. People sometimes fall victim to many of the complications that often arise in life. As landlords (and human beings) we can understand this, as each of us has experienced our own dilemmas.

Just because a person has filed for bankruptcy due to tough circumstances or developed poor credit, this doesn't mean he or she will be a poor tenant. What's important is that the applicant is honest with you and explains why they have bad credit (or filed for bankruptcy). Then, as a landlord you can decide for yourself if they seem genuine and determined to get things turned around.

Remember, a landlord wants to build beneficial business relationship. This starts with a healthy relationship. It doesn't mean you need to be friends with your tenants or do them any favours But if an applicant is honest with you about their sensitive situation it's a good sign, and their honesty may be an excellent sign. In return, you can extend some trust their way, which can be the beginning of an amicable relationship for both landlord and tenant.

You must also consider that an applicant with poor credit can turn out be a great tenant. They may be determined to correct their credit by spending wisely and paying their bills on time. The point is that not all people with poor credit are guaranteed to be bad tenants.

Another benefit of having a tenant with poor credit is that he or she could be a tenant for a long time, which is good for your business. The reasons are simple. First, they might have trouble getting mortgage approval, so they won't be buying a home (and therefore moving out of your property) any time soon. Second, they may have trouble finding other willing landlords because many are scared off by poor credit.

My point here is that *some* prospects with poor credit might be excellent tenants, so you shouldn't disqualify them immediately on the grounds of poor credit. The rules for considering a tenant with poor credit are:

- They are honest and forthright with their credit history
- Their poor credit story is verified by them, the credit report, and references

Please note that I'm not suggesting you should seek out tenants with poor credit or that poor credit is a good sign. I'm merely suggesting that you should consider all scenarios and circumstances as a landlord.

The Proactive Landlord and Story Corroboration

I've just finished telling you that sometimes you should practice understanding with prospects poor credit, but this does not trump the need to always be proactive. This is where story corroboration is important.

An honest 'yes' to the bankruptcy question (or to credit questions) is nowhere near as concerning as a 'no' that turns out to be a 'yes'. If the prospect has been through either, it will be apparent once you cross-reference the applicant's story with the credit report.

It's not a good sign when the prospect tells a lie to start off the relationship. The endgame here is to give the keys to an excellent tenant who will improve your cash flow, grow your equity, and take care of your property. Liars will not help you reach these goals.

In addition to painting a picture of the prospect's credit history, a credit report will also provide you with previous addresses of the applicant. This is another advanced opportunity to corroborate the prospect's story.

Why?

Well, you might notice that some of the addresses listed on the credit report may not have appeared on their application. You might want to consider why a prospect wouldn't include an address on the application? Is it because they broke the lease, were evicted, or had some other conflict with their landlord? They may just be hoping that you won't dig up the truth.

However, you're a proactive landlord, which means you do dig up the truth with your excellent process. If you notice such a discrepancy, ask the applicant about the previously listed address. Did they live there? If so, why didn't they list it? If it was a property they rented, would they provide you with the landlord's contact information?

That's a landlord you want to talk to.

If you call the missing landlord and find out something damaging about the prospect that disqualifies them from becoming your tenant, then you can consider the cost of the credit check to be worthwhile. In fact, catching one liar could be worth 100 credit checks.

You can also corroborate employment information from the credit check, as this information also appears on credit reports. The process and warning signs are exactly the same as with verifying former landlords.

Now, you might be thinking, "Come on Quentin, who would lie about this kind of thing? They must know they will be caught in a lie."

Actually, it's shocking how many people do it, even though it's easy to catch. Many suspects just hope they won't be found out, and who can blame them? There are plenty of reactive landlords to taken advantage of. Most landlords aren't doing credit checks and checking references, which is unfortunate for them, but it's a big advantage for us proactive landlords.

Life Happens – Don't Judge Too Quickly

I learned not to judge tenants' bad credit too quickly when I came across a young blended family who wanted to move into one of my single family homes. The husband and wife were both in their late 20s. The fact it was a blended family is important because the wife's previous marriage was what caused the bad credit in the first place.

The mother in this family had a son from a previous relationship before meeting her new husband. The couple quickly got together after her divorce and had 2 children. It was a tough time for them, and they even moved into the husband's parents' house while they got back on their feet. I found out that they had spent nearly two years working hard, getting back on their feet, getting rid of debt, and (slightly) repairing their credit.

Finally, they were ready to move out on their own and they applied to live in one of my properties. Initially, they passed all the filters, but when it came time for the credit check there were red flags flying all over the place. She had taken out payday loans and not paid them back. R9s were everywhere. It was a mess.

However, the couple was very forthright about her past credit history. They explained everything that happened, and I learned that when she was going through her divorce with her ex-husband, she had no income for a time and was taking care of the young child. Needless to say, she struggled while trying to find childcare, a job, and eventually a place to live when she divorced her husband.

Their forthrightness was important, but even more important was the fact the payday loans report was starting to get old. Nothing negative had happened to her in two years, which gave me every reason to believe that the bad credit history was caused by circumstance. I had good reason to believe she wouldn't let it happen again.

The couple's story made sense, and this is the only true measure you're going to have to be able to verify a tenant with bad credit. If you stick 100% to the book you should never put a tenant with bad credit in one of your properties, but if the story checks out and if there is a bit of history showing that things are turning around, these kinds of tenants can be the best ones.

I approved them to live in the property, and they rewarded me by being excellent tenants. In fact, they were exemplary, even going above the call of duty by fixing a garage door that broke while they were living there. They helped out in other areas, never gave me an ounce of trouble, and moreover paid their rent on time – every time.

It took a while, but after a couple of years as excellent tenants with me, I'm happy to say the couple was able to purchase a home of their own, which means they travelled the long road from being considered a bad credit risk to being a good credit risk.

It's stories like this that make you feel good to be a landlord, but I want to warn you against making helping people your job as a landlord. It's okay to trust tenants with a tough past as long as you have good reason to believe the past is behind them. I had good reason to trust these tenants, so I approved them and it turned out to be a great situation.

Good Credit Vs. Bad Credit

We've just discussed why and how the credit report is valuable for getting more information and corroborating stories, but what about the actual credit rating itself? How do we use the information on the report to improve our decision-making skills?

It's important not to view all credit history the same. There are a variety of flags to look for on a credit check, but not all flags are equal.

For instance, nearly everyone has an overdue *Rogers* or *Bell* bill in their credit history. Sometimes it's because they defaulted, sometimes it's because of a contract dispute with a phone company. As we all know, the only detail cell phone contracts don't mention is the mandatory pain in the butt experience with them. These companies report regularly, but it's not always the individual's fault.

My policy is not to judge too harshly when I see *Rogers* or *Bell* on a credit report. I extend the same leeway for health club memberships that were defaulted on. Some health clubs are almost as bad as the telecom giants, and it's pretty easy to forget about such a payment once you stop going to the health club.

The more serious ones to look for are mortgage, rent, and car payments that came in late or not at all. Living accommodations, transportation costs, and medical bills are top priority when it comes to money management and life planning. There's cause for concern when these aren't maintained and managed properly.

Ultimately, what you want to see on a credit report is that even if an applicant is currently dealing with (or previously had) financial problems that they are making strides and taking the proper steps to deal with their troubles rather than avoiding them. So, if you see "high Rs" from three years ago, but every rating since then has landed in the R1 or R2 range, you know the prospect applicant has been managing their income and bills responsibly for an extended period of time.

On the other hand, if R3s, R4s, R5s (or worse) are scattered all over the report, then you know the applicant has ongoing trouble managing payments and debts and is probably not the right fit for you.

The Decision

So, up until now you've paid for and examined the credit report, analyzed the R ratings, and corroborated the stories. These variables should lead to a 'yes' or a 'no' answer. 'Yes', and applicant is accepted. 'No', and you're still on the search for the right applicant.

It's important to note that you can never be 100% certain that a tenant will be perfect in advance. We work hard and follow an excellent system to minimize risk to the highest degree possible. We have a lot of control through the application of our system, but we are not omnipotent, and if you look for 100% certainty you'll never move. This rule applies in all of business.

What we're looking for is to the best or our abilities and systems to find the right person to start a relationship that will be beneficial to the tenant and to your real estate investment business. This implies risk, but it demands due diligence. Eventually, you just have to make a decision.

The credit report does generate some 'yes' and 'no' answers (for example: an applicant with nonstop R9s and several lies is an automatic no), which can help you to make decisions, but it sometimes generates both 'yes' and 'no'. No matter which kind of answers it gives you, you still have to rely on your own research and intuition for the final decision.

Ultimately, with all the filters you have in place and all the verification, what you want is to try to stay away from the 3% of the tenants that cause 80% of rental problems. This 3% is composed of the dishonest applicants, the potential vandals, and the 'professional tenants'. When you take the necessary steps provided you catch most of those types of applicants. Using these steps, I've never been stuck with a 3 percenter. Once you get through all of the above discussed steps, you're ready to take the final step to turn the applicant into a tenant.

Conditional Acceptance

Once the prospect passes all the filters, you simply ask if they are still interested in the property and willing to move forward and agree to the terms of the lease. If they say yes, you're now in the *conditional acceptance* phase. You then invite them to meet to go over the final terms of the tenancy and the conditions of the lease.

Conditional acceptance means both you and the applicant understand that they will live in your property once all necessary documentation is complete. Conditional

Acceptance is not legally binding Rather, it's more like a handshake agreement between landlord and applicant where both parties know that the conditional handshake will lead to an unconditional legal agreement, once the documentation is signed.

A Final Filter

You should now understand a few key aspects of the Credit Check Filter. This means being able to recognize what the different R ratings mean, and when to treat these ratings as toxic and when to not worry about them.

You should also know that as a landlord you are entering into a business relationship and personal relationship with a tenant, so if they extend trust your way then you can return that trust so long as you believe it is in your best interest.

You also know that when certain information appears on a credit report it's not in your best interest to approve this tenant (Alert: R-9s).

Your ability to read and understand credit reports means you should have a good sense about how reliable your applicant will be when it comes to paying rent, in-full and on time. Once you've given yourself the best chance possible by performing these steps then you can enter into the unconditional acceptance phase with the applicant.

You still don't have a sure-thing tenant though.

The next step in the process will ensure you and the tenant have entered a formal, legal agreement, which will be the official beginning of their tenancy. All the filters in the world are great, but you will still have to deal with the actual tenancy. Having solid legal footing protects both you and your property.

Before you can trust someone with your property, you must make sure every area of your asset is covered with written and signed agreements. Continue to the next chapter for a rundown of all these necessary documents and agreements. This will include an explanation about collecting rent checks, the how and why for each form, and an explanation about how important communication is at this stage.

> "*The Dip creates scarcity;*
> *scarcity creates value*
>
> – SETH GODIN

CHAPTER 6

BRINGING IN THE TENANT

Communication and Clarity

You've safely landed a great tenant then, right? You interviewed them personally, you checked their references, and you did the essential credit checks to make sure that this tenant is willing and able to pay rent on time.

You're almost there.

You're getting close, but you have a big communication job to do before you can hand the keys over to the tenant. Every good relationship starts with communication and clarity, and in this case, explaining to them every feature of the property and all the details of the paperwork they are agreeing to sign. Now you're probably thinking, 'paperwork is awful and a pain to draft. I already have a lease, isn't that enough?' The answer in short is 'N-O'.

You don't want anything left unsaid with your tenant and you don't want to have to explain anything to them or make them agree to anything after they have already taken residence. Such a situation could lead to challenges when it comes to each of your legal rights and that needs to be avoided by any means necessary. The way to do this is simple.

The key here is *communication*. Reciting a laundry list of rules and expectations to a tenant and then having them read through and put their signature on a small stack of paperwork isn't usually exciting, but it's a duty that requires great clarity and diligence on your part.

Here's the list of tasks and forms you'll be aware of and understand by the end of this chapter:

- **The Rent Talk** – this discussion is your final filter to make sure your applicant is ready to become a tenant
- **Rent Cheques** – the first and last month rent cheques are mandatory and need to be submitted ASAP
- **The Lease** – your legal contract with all the necessary terms and conditions
- **The Miscellaneous Documents** – Pet Addendum, New Tenant's Info form, and the "before you get your keys" checklist.
- **Utility Responsibility** – Have the applicant arrange for the utilities to switch over to their name before they move in.

- **Unconditional Acceptance** – This second stage of acceptance will be explained, as well as what to do if your tenant has already signed the lease and changes their mind about moving into the residence.

You want and need all these steps in place to eliminate troublesome gray areas. The more communication between you and the tenant, and the more the tenant understands their rights and responsibilities, the more confident and safe you'll feel once they have the keys and full access to your property.

Rent Talk with Tenant

Just as you would with your daughter's new boyfriend, you need to sit down at the kitchen table for a serious (but not severe) rent talk with the applicant. The purpose is to set expectations and clarify responsibilities, and in many ways can be thought of as one final filter. Like many steps of the important landlord steps, the rent talk isn't complicated, but it is essential.

The importance of the rent talk is to lay it all out before the relationship becomes legally binding. With a clear understanding of responsibilities, some tenants decide to back out. If this happens, it's a good thing, but it's more common that they will still take the place, but just be far more prepared and educated about their responsibilities entering the relationship.

This is why the Rent Talk must be detailed, consistent, and honest. To make sure your rent talk exemplifies these qualities, have the points of the rent talk printed out and ready in an easy to display binder so you can set it down on the table and go over all its points. The visual aid along with getting tenant feedback (and questions) will ensure the tenant understands every component of their tenancy.

Key points of the Rent Talk are:

1. **Congratulations** – Explain to the tenant how much you value their loyalty and business, and that you were pleased with their cooperation and results during the application process. Explain how rigorous your filtration system. Explain that you've done your research, and that you look forward to a successful relationship with them

---

Welcome!

Congratulations!

. YOU are an important part of our business.
. We are proud of our performance & the referrals received —we want your experience to be the same.
. Thanks for choosing us for your housing needs.

---

2. **Mission statement and explanation of the rental agreement** – At this time you can share your landlording standards with your tenant and that you strive to provide quality homes, safe residences, excellent services, and competitive rents. You can also explain the lease in detail at this point.

Our Mission Statement

To provide housing for responsible people who always make their payments on time, take care of their home and property.

We intend to find and keep these people by providing:

. A Quality Home
. Excellent Service
. Safe
. Competitive Rents

What is a Rental Agreement?

The promise from the Landlord to provide a home in good cosmetic shape, with safe mechanical systems for the full term of the rental agreement.

AND

The promise from the Tenant to treat the property with care by maintaining its good condition and paying rent on time for the full term of the rental agreement.

3. **Tenant's Responsibilities** – You must explain to the tenant that they're responsible for maintaining the property in order to avoid costly repairs, comply with all by-laws, condo rules and regulations(if applicable), and must follow the terms and conditions set out in the lease agreement. Explain how this benefits both parties.

Your Responsibilities

Congratulations on your move into a single family townhome! You have maintenance responsibilities with your home for the full term of the rental agreement.

Your responsibility is to:
- help maintain your home in good condition and prevent costly repairs.
- comply with all the By-laws of the Condominium Corporation.
- follow the terms and conditions set out in the Lease agreement.

This equals affordable rent for YOU.

Remember, we are responsible for these mechanical systems: HVAC, Hot Water Heater, Water Supply, Smoke Detectors.

---

4. **Maintenance guarantee and repair request information** – You want your tenant to be knowledgeable about the property's physical attributes as well as the lease. Go over the household mechanical systems and appliances the landlord is responsible for. Explain that things can only be fixed if the tenant cooperates and informs the landlord of repairs. Provide

phone numbers for the tenant to call in case of certain repairs. Explain that maintenance calls will be operated through the Grasshopper phone service. Explain that you don't immediately respond to maintenance requests, but that you respond in a timely manner. Explain the difference between routine maintenance and emergency. Provide an *emergency* number in case of fire, flood, or safety hazards.

Maintenance Guarantee

We are responsible for the mechanical systems in your residence, and promise to maintain them in good working order for the full term of your rental agreement.

We employ professional, friendly service people and utilize several licensed trade professionals to service your home.

We understand that many people complain about the timeliness of their Landlord's repairs; however we can not repair something that we know nothing about ... please contact us.

Maintenance Requests

If you have a maintenance request, you have a few choices:

1. Call our office at **1-877-XXX-XXXX** and **press 2.** A copy of your voicemail will be kept for our records.

2. Fax in the Maintenance Request form included in your Tenant Handbook   to **1-877-XXX-XXXX**.

3. Go to our web site and submit a Maintenance Request online. (www   .YourWebSite.ca)

In An Emergency

In an emergency, for example flooding, fires, or a safety hazard, please contact **1-877-XXX-XXXX** and **press 3** as soon as possible. You call will be given the highest priority.

5. **Rent Dues** - Explain that you run a business and that the tenant's financial obligations are taken seriously. Explain that there is zero tolerance for late rent payments, which means that a late rent payment will result in immediate action.

Paying Rents

We're NOT cold and mean people, however we are in the business world:

Financial obligations are taken seriously; unfortunately with ZERO TOLERANCE for excuses.

Notice To End a Tenancy Early For Non-payment of Rent
Form N4

To: (Tenant's name)	From: (Landlord's name)

This is a legal notice that could lead to you being evicted from your home.

Address of the Rental Unit

Street Number   Street Name

Street Type (e.g. Street, Avenue, Road)   Direction (e.g. East)   Unit/Apt./Suite

Municipality (city, town, etc.)   Province   Postal Code
O N

This information is from your landlord:

I am giving you this notice because I believe you owe me $ ____ , ____ . ____ in rent.

See the table on the next page for the details about how I calculated this amount.

I can apply to the Landlord and Tenant Board to have you evicted if you do not:

- pay this amount* by ____ / ____ / ____   This date is called the **termination date**.
  dd   mm   yyyy
or
- move out by the termination date

* If another rent payment comes due on or before the date you make the above payment to your landlord, you must also pay this extra amount.

WHAT YOU NEED TO KNOW
The following information is provided by the Landlord and Tenant Board

The termination date
The date that the landlord gives you in this notice to pay or move out must be at least:
- 14 days after the landlord gives you the notice, if you rent by the month or year, or
- 7 days after the landlord gives you the notice, if you rent by the day or week.

What if you agree with the notice
If you agree that you owe the amount that the landlord is claiming, you should pay this amount by the termination date in this notice. If you do so, this notice becomes void and the landlord cannot apply to the Board to evict you. If you do not pay the amount owing, and the landlord applies to the Board to evict you, you will likely have to pay the landlord's filing fee of $170.00, plus what you owe.

If you move out by the date in this notice, your tenancy will end on the termination date. However, you may still owe money to your landlord. Your landlord will not be able to apply to the Board but they may still take you to Court for this money.

What if you disagree with the notice
If you disagree with what the landlord has put in this notice, you do not have to move out. You could talk to your landlord. You may also want to get legal advice. If you cannot work things out, and the landlord applies to the Board, you will be able to go to a hearing and explain why you disagree.

10101

Version. 15/10/2009   This form has been approved by the Landlord and Tenant Board   Page 1 of 2

6. All-Star Tenant Program – You may wish to include an All-Star Tenant Program, if so now is the time to explain. This can act as a valuable incentive for excellent tenant behaviour and may help you get renter referrals from your best tenants. Explain any rewards programs or referral fees you pay for excellent tenants. I offer $200 to anyone who refers me a tenant that I end up signing.

At the conclusion of the rent talk, the tenant will be fully aware of everything they are agreeing to, and hopefully will be delighted with the level of transparency and diligence you've provided.

Forms, Deposits, and Duties

After the heart-to-heart, known as the Rent Talk, it's time to get down to the nitty-gritty of forms, legalities, and payments. Below is an explanation and description of all the mandatory forms and payments that need to be completed by the soon-to-be tenant.

First and Last Month's Rent – Signing a lease is great, but the rule of move-ins is that *nobody moves in without paying first and last month's rent*. Payment serves as your protection in case you end up with a flaky tenant that wants to back out of tenancy on the first day of the month, or anything else. You have every right to keep the first month's rent while you search for another tenant, but without that money in the bank you don't stand a chance.

Ensure that you only accept certified cheques, email money transfers, or money orders for the first and last month's rent. At this point you don't have a history with the tenant, so it's best to get another layer of protection in the form of cheque certification or money order.

All money in and out must be tracked (as discussed in *The Property Management Toolbox: A How to Guide for Ontario Real Estate Investors and Landlords)*. Taking a cheque from the tenant at this stage creates the following important paper trail:

- Tenant who wrote the cheque should keep their own personal record after they have written you a cheque
- A bank record after you deposit the cheque to your account
- A bank record of the funds coming out of the tenant's account
- A company receipt to give to the applicant
- You will keep a copy of the company receipt for your own files
- Always deposit these cheques immediately.

Sign the Lease Agreement

The lease needs to be signed by both parties, state the dates of the beginning and end of the lease, state the terms of the lease, state the address of the property for rent, and list all the involved parties. The terms and conditions on the lease must be detailed and concise so that there are no gray areas.

In addition, ensure you include any additional terms, conditions, or addendums that apply to the specific property. The contract itself could be the topic of another book, but for our purposes here, I will just discuss one special addendum.

Pet Addendum

Tenants' pet rights are robust, and it can put landlords in a vulnerable situation. Let me explain.

A landlord can disallow a rental if they know that a tenant has pets and if they don't want a tenant with pets in their property. However, if a tenant moves in first, and then brings a pet into the property after, there is almost nothing a landlord can do about this.

These rules don't necessarily make much sense (as a landlord speaking), but these are the cards we've been dealt.

The few tenants that are aware of this loophole (and who take advantage of it by pretending not to have a pet before bringing it in later) are generally rather troublesome, which makes sense if you think about it. I mean, before they've even moved in they've already lied about not having a pet – it's a sign of a potential 3 percenter.

Unfortunately, as landlords our hands are tied. If a tenant brings a pet in a Pet Addendum is a way to pre-emptively deal with any problem that might arise. Any tenant that brings in a pet signs it.

A Pet Addendum states that if a pet in the residence causes any damages and/or any repair costs to the property that the tenant will be responsible for the damage and the cost of the repairs. It goes on to state that if the pet were to harm any visitors – landlords, maintenance workers, guests – then the tenant will be liable for any damages.

Make every tenant sign a Pet Addendum. This way, if a pet does happen to appear after move-in, at least you are covered should the pet result in any damages or other problems.

Pets – The Alternative Approach

I've just finished telling you to make sure you get a pet addendum in order to protect yourself against the potential of a pet (especially a dog) damaging your property. This is the approach I take, and I generally prefer not to have pets in my properties if I can. I find that even if they don't cause major damage the wear and tear is sped up enough by their presence that it's better not to have them.

However, there are others who actively court dog owners as tenants. This might sound crazy considering the problems just mentioned above, but what if I told you they still protect themselves with the Pet Addendum in the lease, and then on top of that charge a premium on the rent?

It might not be such a crazy idea after all, as some of the landlords I've spoken to have been able to charge as much as $100 more per month to be a 'pet friendly house'. At the end of the day, you will have to make a judgment call whether or not the risk is worth it and the protection against the risk is robust enough.

Just to be clear, I am not saying that a prospective landlord adds $50 to the rent because a tenant is bringing in a pet. They just set their rent $50 higher than other landlords with similar properties, and advertise their rental at that price.

To come to a good decision it would be worthwhile to consider the cost of normal wear and tear with a dog in the property. Ask what parts of the home might be ruined and how much it would cost.

If you can replace the excess wear and tear in the property for $1200 for example, but you're charging a $50 monthly premium, focusing on the pet market might be a wise strategic decision.

The other big advantage to going after the dog owner market is being even more niched in your tenant and property selection. If you chose to go this route, you could even run two ads, one targeting dog owners, and another targeting families.

Dog owners are often very committed to their pets. They literally arrange their lifestyle around their dogs, and any marketing that speaks directly to their needs has potential to work.

Information for New Tenants Form

The *Information for New Tenants* Form is a standard form created by the Landlord and Tenant Board. Make two copies and have the tenant sign and date both. Then keep one for your own records and give one to the tenant for them to keep in their records.

Covered in this from are rent responsibilities, rent increases, door locks, deposits, privacy privileges, contact information, and more. This is a valuable form for two reasons.

1. It outlines all the basic and most significant rights and responsibilities of landlords and tenants in simple and easy to understand terms. While your Lease will out of necessity contain a large amount of legal jargon, the *Information for New Tenants* form is straightforward and leaves very little open for interpretation.

2. Should any issues ever arise with a tenant and these issues are presented to the Landlord and Tenant Board, the existence of this form will be vital to your case. The tenant will have read and signed a copy of the *Information for New Tenants* form, which you keep in your records. Your copy will demonstrate to the Board that the tenant was made explicitly aware of many landlord and tenant rules and regulations and it will prevent any chance for the tenant to claim ignorance.

Give Tenant the 'Before You Get Your Keys Checklist'

This is a checklist to help the tenant stay organized and assist them in their move. It's a simple set of instructions that reminds the tenant to do some things that they probably otherwise wouldn't. It instructs them to:

- Contact the post office and have mail forwarded to the new address
- If needed, book a moving truck well in advance
- Present a copy of your tenant insurance policy before the move-in date
- Have the utilities switched over to your name (more in next point)
- Etc.

These might seem obvious to some, but there is great benefit in providing this. Who hasn't forgotten a seemingly important to-do list item when busy with so many other things? We all have, but this checklist puts all the dates and minor duties that the tenant needs to complete in one easy place.

Many tenants will have already considered and planned for these items, but this checklist isn't for them. It's for the tenant whose strengths aren't necessarily to plan ahead and take care of all the tedious administrative details. By presenting them with list, you're helping your tenant be prepared. It gives you one less thing to worry about, and shows tenants a high level of care.

Transfer of Utilities and Utilities Agreement Form

As you will have mentioned in the checklist, the tenant has to call the utilities providers to get the utilities in their name starting on move-in day. Under no circumstance do you want a tenant to be in your property until they have assumed responsibility of the utilities. Remove any chance of being stuck with utilities bills in your name. Make sure this gets done.

In addition to reminding tenants to get utilities in their own name, you must also have them sign Landlords a *Utility Agreement* form, which states that a landlord is allowed to discuss the tenant's utility account with the utilities provider. The agreement will also state that the landlord does not have the authority to disconnect or interrupt utility services. This form also outlines privacy terms and responsibilities when it comes to providing future forward addresses.

Once the tenant has gotten the utilities switched over, ask them to call and notify you that it has been done.

Unconditional Acceptance

Unconditional acceptance is in place after you receive certified first and last month's rent, the utilities are transferred over, and the lease is signed (and other paperwork complete).

At this point, there is a slight chance that the tenant backs out, which is what we'll discuss next.

Dealing With an Applicant That Backs Out

This is not a pleasant scenario. While the applicant has formally entered into a legal agreement, they still have not physically lived there, which makes this a gray area. The landlord still has responsibilities to the applicant in this scenario.

Now, you might be tempted to draw a hard line. You could say to the tenant, "Tough luck, you already agreed and provided payment, so you're committed to living in the residence and paying all rent payments through the length of the lease. The tenant may then decide they don't want to challenge or question you and move in instead.

If this is your approach, you might want to ask yourself, "Is this really an ideal situation for anyone involved?" If you draw a hard line it will not be a good start to the relationship, and you will end up with a tenant that doesn't want to live in your property. I don't recommend this approach. This is a risky when trying to build a relationship and will likely end in bitterness, then to make matters worse, you'll be stuck with a tenant who will never give you the benefit of the doubt.

Another risk of the hard line approach is that the applicant may determine they're not yet fully obligated to the contractual demands and challenge your authority on the matter. They may have legitimate grounds for a challenge since they haven't yet taken residence.

In this case, either you or the tenant can bring the issue to the Landlord Tenant Board. You may win at the Board, but there is no chance the process will be worth your time. A resolution will not come quickly, and the Board generally leans in favour of the tenant's rights.

I would suggest a more accommodating approach to this problem. If a tenant backs out, just explain to them that you understand their decision but that you will have to hold them accountable for the property until you have another tenant lined-up and ready to take over the property. This approach isn't as abrupt as the first and has a number of benefits for the landlord.

To mitigate this, I suggest always marketing and advertising the property with your normal system until the tenant is moved in. If a tenant then backs out and you agree with them to keep looking for a tenant, you can then field calls, utilize the filtration system, and take immediate action to find another worthy tenant. If you've shut down the marketing, you will always have a bit of a lag before finding a suitable tenant.

You should have received the applicant's first and last month's rent, so you can cover any time or costs lost while searching for another tenant. Hopefully you don't have to do this, but it may happen because as a proactive landlord you will not slam any old tenant into the property. Just because you're trying to accommodate the tenant, doesn't mean you can take a break from diligence. On the contrary, this is the time to be extra diligent.

Another benefit of the softer approach is that you're not forcing someone to live in a situation they don't feel is right for them. I know many landlords despise the tenant turnover process and will avoid it at all costs, but trying to force an applicant/tenant to do something they aren't sure about means starting a relationship on the wrong foot, which will only cause you stress and waste your time.

Find and build the right relationship, and don't force someone into a non-committed relationship just because you feel like someone took advantage of your time and an opportunity. Move on quickly, put your filters to use once again and keep working with diligence and process to find the right fit.

Communication and Clarity – The Result

If you've gotten this far on your process, you finally have a tenant that's ready to move in. You have communicated to them everything they need to know. They understand the terms of the lease, have submitted their first and last month's rent, are aware of all the pet and utilities details, and they know they have a clear, consistent, and trustworthy landlord.

This is good for tenants, and after finishing this process you can feel confident that your property is in the hands of a well-prepared tenant. In the rare case that a tenant (that has been through your filtration system) turns out to be troublesome, you're still in good shape because you've covered all your bases. And you did it all thanks to diligence, clarity, and communication.

Now it's finally time to move to the final phase and tie up the loose ends.

You need to be aware of the closing procedures and finishing touches contained in the next chapter. Without these you might sabotage all of the hard work you've done up to this point. To finish the job you need to ensure you're on the same page with your tenant in every way, which when done properly also helps you prepare for the inevitable move-out. Read on to learn about this vital next step.

There is no place like home

– L. Frank Baum,
The Wonderful Wizard of Oz

CHAPTER 7

TENANT MEETS HOME

Almost There

It's time to turn your property into a new home - to make your fully qualified applicant into a full-blown tenant. You've officially reached the homestretch of the vacancy filling process.

Some great questions to ask here might be, "What are the procedures for that last walkthrough? Is there anything I'm forgetting? What final steps can I take to make sure my assets are covered in the event that some unforeseen circumstances arise? How do I make my new tenant know that I appreciate their business and that I'm looking forward to starting our new relationship?"

This chapter puts the finishing touches on your knowledge, and you should feel confident to execute on the vacancy filling process after reading. You should be able to rest easy after this chapter knowing your adherence to the system has paid off. Here's a brief list of what to expect in this chapter and in that last stretch before your property is also your tenant's new home:

- *Take pictures* of your property so there is no chance for any misunderstanding about what the residence looked like before the tenant moved in.

- *Verify* that the *utilities* have been/will be switched over by calling the utility providers, and make sure you get a copy of the tenant's *proof of insurance.*

- Set a date and time for the *move-in inspection* and arrive prepared.

- Complete the *Accommodation Inspection Report* during the final walkthrough.

- Compile and present the tenant with the *Tenant's Handbook.*

- Arrange when and where the tenant will receive their *keys*.

- Give the tenant a *warm welcome* to their new home.

- *Celebrate!*

Read on, learn up, and finish strong.

Turn an Applicant into a Tenant

You've made it to the final step. Now, you must verify a couple of things and conduct the move-in inspection to turn your unconditionally accepted applicant into your newest tenant.

Confirmation Call and Copy of Insurance Liability

In the previous chapter I explained that after the tenant transfers over the utilities that they need to call and notify you that it has been done. Once they have done this and before the move-in inspection, call the utility company and confirm that this has been done. It's great to hear it's been done from the tenant, but it's much better to verify it directly with the utilities companies.

If the transfer has not been done, stop with everything else related to the property and contact the tenant to find out why it hasn't been done. If they'd told you it was done but it's not, you need to get to the bottom of it right away. No matter how trustworthy a tenant seems, never forget that you are in a business and that when something seems awry you need to act immediately. Make sure utilities are under the tenant's name before you let them move in.

Just as utilities have to be verified, so does the tenant's insurance liability forms. Tenants must have renter's insurance in place before they move into your property. This is a gray area of renting properties. What would happen if there were a fire, flood, or another catastrophe? Would your insurance cover the tenant? If so, would it affect your premiums? Also let them know that your insurance does not cover the tenant's contents or a place for them to stay if there is a fire, flood, or other disaster.

It's not a wise policy to leave this up to chance. Make sure the tenant is covered under their own tenant insurance before letting them move in. You need to verify it before they move in, and if they don't have it just before the move-in takes place you're exposed. Stop everything and figure it out immediately.

This confirmation call is a small but vital step of your system. Skipping this step opens the door for unwanted risk. Once these matters are confirmed, it's time to schedule a move-in inspection with the tenant.

Almost there!

A Picture is Worth a Thousand Dollars

Before we discuss the move-in inspection, I'd like to take a moment to stress the importance of photos at this point in the process,

Move in day is time to get your camera out. I'd like you to think way back to the first chapter when we discussed the preparation steps taken when the tenant gives notice to vacate. You might remember that part of the process is to discuss damage with outgoing tenants. To have a well-informed discussion (proof) with the outgoing tenants about damage you must be well prepared with photos.

These are the same photos you will use on your move-in inspection. Each stage of landlording is connected. To have a successful move-out, you need to take targeted action at move-in. Photos at move-in gives you vital proof for move-out. Focus your photos on the following areas:

- Floors and walls in high traffic areas (hallways, foyers, landings, stairs)
- Appliances (inside of the fridge, inside and outside stove/oven)
- Cupboard doors and countertops
- Showers and bath tubs
- Linoleum, hardwood, laminate floors
- Light fixtures
- Patio doors
- Carbon dioxide and smoke detectors
- Every bedroom

Before the move-in inspection get a set of these pictures printed and bring them to the move-in inspection. Then during the move-inspection, you will walk through the property with the new tenants and show them a picture and the actual spot or item that is in the picture. After the tenant confirms that the pictures represents the current state of that spot, and then have them sign the back of the picture. Then once the tenant has signed it put a stamp with the date near their signature.

If the tenant causes any damage beyond the regular and expected wear and tear to any part of the property then you can refer to these pictures to demonstrate the extent of the damage compared with how it looked when the tenant first moved in. Having these pictures will minimize any chance for disagreement about the condition of the property later. In effect, it disallows them from saying, "Oh, that was like that before we moved in."

You probably noticed that the areas to focus on are areas where, not only is damage the most likely to occur, but also where the highest cost of repairs would occur. A wall with a few dings is easy and inexpensive to fix, and likely to occur over the time of a tenant's residency. In other words, it's normal wear and tear. This isn't the same as evidence of neglect and recklessness to the more permanent and expensive fixtures.

Flooring that needs to be replaced because it's stained and gouged is both costly and time-consuming to replace. A stovetop that has excessive burns and is permanently damaged is not acceptable. The same can be said for cupboards with knife divots. If you're new to landlording, these kinds of damages might sound unlikely, but these all happen and they leave a large dent in your wallet.

These kinds of damages don't just come from 3 percenters, either. Even relatively good tenants can cause this type of damage. A lot of tenants are careless and lazy when it comes to cleaning, cooking, and moving furniture.

Even great tenants aren't as keen as the landlord is about maintaining the quality and cleanliness of the property. This can result in anywhere from moderate to extensive damage, and if you don't have photo documentation the cost will fall upon you later. Take the photos, have them printed, have the tenants sign off on them, and then keep them safe. This step is vital for your business. Do not skip this step.

If A Tenant Causes Damage to A Property

Date: August 28th, 20XX

Mr. Thomas Tenant, 222 Maple Street,
Whitby, Ontario
B2B 2B2

Dear Mr. Tenant:

As you're already aware, on August 14th we had a contractor complete the following repair: Describe the Repair

This repair was identified as being caused by improper use of the _____.

The Residential Tenancies Act states the following:

34. The tenant is responsible for the repair of undue damage to the rental unit or residential complex caused by the wilful or negligent conduct of the tenant, another occupant of the rental unit or a person permitted in the residential complex by the tenant. 2006, c. 17, s. 34.

Please pay the attached bill within 30 days.

Sincerely,

Name of Landlord

Conduct the Move-In Inspection/
Final Walkthrough

Now your property transforms into the tenant's home. It's also the chance to explain to the tenant the significant and subtle details they need to know in order to manage and maintain their new home properly.

When they walked through for the first time (back when you weren't even sure if they were a suspect or a prospect) wasn't the time to discuss all of the finer details. If you were doing your job properly during the first showing, it means you were asking questions and trying to figure out if they were a good tenant or not. You were also likely trying to sell the tenant on your property by focusing their attention on the benefits of living there.

This move-in walkthrough is a different process than the original walkthrough. Here is a step-by-step process for how to prepare for and conduct your final inspection:

1. Schedule the Walkthrough – Set a time and date to meet the tenant at your property. The date will be dependent on when the last tenant moved-out and when the move-in date is. Ideally, it would be two or three days before move-in and the residence would be completely empty. That's not always possible so just plan and keep everyone informed as best as you can. There's a good chance this will happen on their move-in day.

2. Bring necessary materials – This includes the Accommodation Inspection Report (more on this in point 8), the Tenant Handbook (more in this in point 9), the pictures you took of the property, and the appliance manuals.

3. Utility controls – Show the tenant where the shut-offs for all taps are (interior and exterior if applicable), where the electrical panel is, and where any meters are and how to read them in the case the tenant would have to do their own meter readings. Communicate to them that if they have any trouble or uncertainties in the future about using any of these controls that they should not hesitate to contact you or your maintenance team. Explain that it takes much less time and money for you to answer a quick question about how the utilities work than repair accidents that might occur if the tenant is unsure about their functions and mistakenly misuses them.

4. Alarms and detectors – Point out where the smoke alarms and CO_2 detectors are. Demonstrate that they're in good working order and have the tenant sign-off on the location and condition of them. Not doing this could be the most costly mistake you ever make. I think we'd all agree that the worst thing that could ever happen in one of our properties is a death. This step could literally save a life and save you from any liability from a death.

5. Appliances – As mentioned above, you will have brought along all appliance manuals. Demonstrate to the tenant that they are all in working order and ask them to refer to the manual if they are unsure of any appliances features. These include the fridge, the range, the washer and dryer, and the dishwasher if there is one present at the property.

6. Garage door – Show the tenant how the automatic garage door opener works. Also show them how and when to use the override key in case the mechanical opener isn't working and there is no access through a man-door to get in the garage.

Next...

Complete the Accommodation Inspection Report

For the move-in inspection you'll need the *Accommodation Inspection Report*. This report is a detailed and organized list of anything and everything contained on the inside and outside of the property – light fixtures, fans, doors, fences, gates, toilets, sinks, etc.

ACCOMODATION INSPECTION REPORT

Address of Rental Premises:					Name of Landlord:			
Name of Tenant:					Name of Tenant:			
Name of Tenant:					Name of Tenant:			

Inspections should be conducted when premises are vacant unless the landlord and tenant or their agents otherwise agree.

	IN CONDITION				OUT CONDITION			
KEYS	Number of keys for premises			Mailbox	Number of keys returned for premises			Mailbox
ENTRANCE	OK	Needs Repair	Needs Cleaning	Description	OK	Needs Repair	Needs Cleaning	Description
Doors, Closets								
Walls, Trim								
Floor covering								
Ceiling								
Windows, Screens								
Electrical fixtures								
Other								
Other								
KITCHEN	OK	Needs Repair	Needs Cleaning	Description	OK	Needs Repair	Needs Cleaning	Description
Walls, Trim								
Floor covering								
Ceiling								
Countertops, Sinks								
Cupboards, Doors								
Stove/Hood								
Fridge								
Dishwasher								
Windows, Screens								
Electrical fixtures								
Other								
Other								
LIVING/DINING ROOM	OK	Needs Repair	Needs Cleaning	Description	OK	Needs Repair	Needs Cleaning	Description
Walls, Trim								
Floor covering								
Ceiling								
Closets, Doors								
Drapes, Rods								
Windows, Screens								
Electrical fixtures								
Other								
Other								
BEDROOM 1	OK	Needs Repair	Needs Cleaning	Description	OK	Needs Repair	Needs Cleaning	Description
Walls, Trim								
Floor covering								
Ceiling								
Closets, Doors								
Drapes, Rods								
Windows, Screens								
Electrical fixtures								
Other								

Together with the tenant you will tour through the entire property and mark down on the *Accommodation Inspection Report* any findings that you come across during the walkthrough. Anything that appears damaged or out the ordinary must be noted in the report and a photo must be taken.

Typically, this will be something noticeable and slightly damaged but that isn't crucial enough to call for a renovation to repair it. Slightly cracked tiles in the bathroom, or random cigarette burns on a carpet are examples of items you may find and note on the report.

As you tour the property room-by-room, point out any findings to the tenant and mark them down on your *Accommodation Inspection Report*. Have the tenant initial next to your indication and description of the finding.

Also, have the tenant help you with this process. If they notice anything that you didn't, ask them to mention it so you can mark them down. Having them fully engaged helps remove problems later. They have to sign off on the report saying they approve the report. Anything missing from the report will considered their damage on move-out, so it's important they take an active role in the process.

One more note: as mentioned above, the walkthrough is also the time to get the tenants to sign off on the photos so there is verified photo evidence about the state of the property.

Once finished, make a copy of the *Accommodation Inspection Report* to give to your tenant. Take your original copy and place it in the tenant's new red folder along with their Lease, Utility Agreement, Information for New Tenant form, Pet Addendum, receipts, and any other documents you collected along the way.

Ahhh. There. I feel much better having my ducks in a row, don't you? Anyone would agree it's a beautifully systematized landlord circle we just travelled together? From reviewing the outgoing tenant's red folder to starting the new tenant's red folder, it's been a long journey (although the actual process won't take as long it seems by reading the whole book), and now this tenant is officially in the property, but there is still a bit more work to do.

Present and Review the Tenant Handbook

The Tenant Handbook sounds diminutive and cute, but it's actually a hefty binder that you assemble for each tenant. Everything you've explained to them, taught them, and warned then against can be found in this document. It sets the ground rules for an effective tenancy and it contains heaps of helpful, indispensable, and mandatory information. Oh, and it might never be looked at. Some tenants ignore it, but others actually use it.

More importantly, it will have important documents and information that *will* help you at some point during tenancy. Imagine the difference between directing a tenant to their binder to learn how to work the oven versus you going over there to show them. It can be a real time saver – for a lot more complex issues than the oven, too.

By the time you present the tenant with their handbook you'll have already taught them plenty throughout the process, now's a chance to reinforce it one last time. Have I mentioned we need to train our tenants?

The contents of the handbook/binder include a copy of their signed lease, an explanation for why they need liability insurance, contact information for several important people including yourself, water meter reading instructions, and so on. The handbook also contains many important notes, provisions and requirements that will prove to be very useful:

- **Essentials Info**:
  - A move-out checklist with all expectations when it comes to cleaning and taking proper action when ending the tenancy

- Any condo rules and regulations if the residency is in a condominium
- Instructions on how to bag, tag, and ensure proper removal of garbage.
- Etc.
- **Helpful Hints:**
  - Reminder/notice that tenants can claim moving expenses with Revenue Canada and where to access the form.
  - A guide on how to cut down on energy costs by using efficient light bulbs, improving air circulation, and how to exercise common sense when it comes to opening and closing windows throughout both the day and the seasons
  - Pest Control guide that explains how to keep the residence free of bugs and rodents that will compromise the cleanliness and quality of the home.
  - Etc.

- **Safety/Survival tips**
  - What to do if there is suddenly and interruption to the utilities
  - What to do in the case there is a fire (specifically in the garage).
  - Etc.

As always, refer to www.theontariolandlordtoolbox.
com for all resources, including the contents of the
handbook. If you're not currently using a tenant handbook,
I highly recommend you do.

Every ounce of information in the handbook should be
useful to a tenant. Some of it is only used for worst-case
scenarios, but if the worst-case scenario arises it sure is a
lot more helpful if the tenant has made herself aware and
familiar with this information and keeps it readily available.
This is why I recommend going through the binder with
them rather than just handing it over. In an emergency
situation (or even a regular situation), they might not know
what to do, but they may just remember one thing – that
you told them to look in the binder.

Encourage your tenant to pour over this manual even
after you review it with them and request that they keep
it in a place where they can access it quickly and regularly.
A tenant that follows this advice and treats the handbook
with the attention and recognition it deserves will in some
ways be as valuable to a landlord as the actual property.
Also mention to the tenant that once their tenancy is over,
it's mandatory they return the handbook. This is a valuable
document, so take care of it.

Keys Please

So, it's time to finally transfer full trust to your tenant
and give them keys to their new home. With these keys,
reassure the tenant that all of the home's locks have been
changed and this is a brand new set of keys exclusive to only
them.

To systematize key distribution, you may use electronic lockboxes placed outside the residence. You can then automate move-in time. You don't even necessarily have to be there –assuming the walk-through takes place prior to the move-in date.

Then, you can simply email the lockbox code to the tenant, so they may move in. This system saves them from waiting on me to bring them keys and saves me from having to rush or worry about getting them their keys.

A Warm Welcome

Hopefully you've gotten this far with an excellent relationship in place – having clear expectations and working together. There is nothing better for a landlord than having an excellent relationship with their tenant.

It's far more important to have communication and clear expectations than to focus on giving gifts, but gifts don't hurt either. I recommend giving each tenant a nice little gift. It doesn't have to be extravagant or over-the-top, though. It's just something that shows you value and appreciate their business and that you want them to be comfortable, calm, and happy in their new home.

A few examples of nice little gifts are plants, a gift certificate to a local business, or even flowers add a pleasant and vibrant touch when they first move-in. The key is to make it something warm and simple but at the same time meaningful.

Celebrate

There is just one final step to make after all that's been done, and it has nothing to do with the tenant, systems, or even work. It's about giving hearty congratulations to you, the landlord. This process is thorough, and if you're not accustomed to landlording this way, it might seem like a lot of work.

There are two positive points to consider. First, it will get easier and easier with each successive time you do it. Second, it might be thorough, but you will save yourself from experiencing so many bigger problems that you're actually saving on a ton of work over the long haul.

You can reflect on these facts as you celebrate your success at completing the entire system, but whatever you think about, just celebrate. This serves an important psychological function as your brain learns to subconsciously associate these little celebrations with success and following the system.

There may come a day when your celebrations get smaller as the process becomes easier and easier. I mean, you might have clapped and cheered the first time you tied your own shoes, but eventually this gets easy and you need a new challenge. This is no different, but with each early success it's vital to celebrate the completion and the success.

This process will make a significant difference to your business, your wealth, and your enjoyment of life, so feel free to celebrate with something meaningful to you.

Get Ready to Do it Again

Hopefully, with a great vacancies and overall landlording system in place, you will have a growing portfolio of properties, which means you will be doing this process over again. I hope you enjoyed your celebration because it's time to get back to work.

It's probably a good idea to go back through all of these steps for the first few vacancies you fill with this process. Make sure the information sinks in to become knowledge. Sure, you'll grow to put your own twists on the system, and you might improve greatly on what you have read here. I commend you if this is the case, and I encourage you to share your own tweaks by attending one of my Durham Real Estate Investing Club meetings, or just email me at info@theontariolandlordtoolbox.com. I'm always looking for improvements to my own system.

With the knowledge and guidance provided throughout this book you have all the tools to be a systematized, proactive, pro-communication, and time-efficient landlord. However, all of the knowledge in the world is no good without real world application. I implore you to implement everything you've learned here, so you can go out there and make a difference in the rental game and in your own life.

Good luck my fellow landlords.

"

I must create a system,
or be enslaved by another
man's. I will not reason
and compare: my business is
to create.

– WILLIAM BLAKE

THE SYSTEM SAVES THE DAY

Systems, Systems, Systems

My intent with writing this book was not to be subtle. If you took the time to search you'd undoubtedly find that the most commonly used word in the book is "system" or some derivation of it.

In truth, landlording success is a combination of systems and relationships. These are the main components to landlording success. Relationships are perhaps a bit tougher to teach. You must bring a sincere attitude for mutual success to every interaction. I covered this topic in more detail in *The Property Management Toolbox: A How to Guide for Ontario Real Estate Investors and Landlords*.

This book was largely an exploration of systems – in particular one large system for filling vacancies. Every step of the system you've just learned about was designed to quickly, efficiently, and effectively fill vacancies.

There may be some things in life worth reinventing every time, but for everything else there are systems. Even Vincent Van Gogh didn't reinvent his brushstroke each time. He had a system for applying paint, and no matter how micro - even creating art is systematic.

I don't know if I want to compare filling vacancies in residential real estate with one of the greatest artists in the world, but the point is that it doesn't make sense to reinvent how you do things every time.

But here's the real truth about systems. You will use a system no matter what. The real question is whether or not you're using the right one. If you've been investing (and landlording) for a while you can find out if your system is working by your level of fatigue, frustration, and comfort.

Managing a few – even up to 50 properties – should be manageable while holding down a full time job. But this is only possible if your entire overall property management system is working well. Filling vacancies is one of the biggest components of the overall landlording system, which is why I'm giving it such special attention to it here.

I'd like to leave you with one story that demonstrates the power of the system you just learned about. As you read through this story, please keep in mind that small things add up when investing in real estate. The story tells about the success of the system in one instance. What would the sum total of successes be for the system if applied over a decade and 10 properties?

The difference is huge. In fact, it can be difficult to grasp how much of a difference the same small set of actions over and over can make.

Real World Example

Just like everyone else, I didn't know much when I started, but I was lucky enough to have been exposed to some excellent mentors along the way, and through the experience of meeting a lot of highly experienced landlords I've learned a lot over the years.

These days, not much gets past me, but even with the help of those mentors in the early days I still suffered the odd landlording nightmare (see earlier story about students in non-student housing). The truth is that even today, there is a chance that a horrible tenant might slip past my system. No system is foolproof. Even Apple and Google create some duds.

It hasn't happened in quite some time, though, because I've learned that following process leads to real results. The combined knowledge I learned from my mentors and fellow investors along with the lessons I've learned by having my feet on the ground, practicing and perfecting the craft of landlording.

In addition to having avoided bad tenants for a while, I rarely have any vacancies or disputes about damage, etc. On the rare occasion that a dispute does arise, I'm generally well prepared with evidence. You see the results of process and system in a thousand small ways every day of landlording. Not too long ago, I carried out a vacancy filling process that illustrated these facts perfectly.

It started out just like any other vacancy filling process. First, I received notice from the outgoing tenant that they were moving out of the townhouse property (in Pickering, Ontario), which caused me to undertake the initial preparations. I then prepared for renovations before kicking the marketing system into gear and showing the property. I expected to get the tenant rented right away without a gap between the outgoing and incoming tenants.

Before long, I started receiving calls, showing the property, and using my normal processes for screening tenants. In this case I was lucky enough to be able to get into the property to do some renovations, which meant there was work ongoing as I was showing the property.

Admittedly, there was a bit of dust throughout the property, but I had warned all of the prospective tenants about this and took care to explain what work would be done and how the property would look when I was finished.

One of the first prospects that came along was a lady that seemed qualified. My first warning sign with her was that she took great pains to point out how dusty and dirty the property was. She was complaining! This shocked me because I'd explained to her that the property would be dirty from renovations well in advance.

A complainer that early in the process is a definite warning sign, but it's a mild enough sign that I would need more evidence to disqualify her. In spite of the dust, she was still interested in the property, and she told me she would like to move forward and apply for tenancy.

So, I gave her an application form and had a pleasant discussion with her. After she left I filed the application away for later review (at a time I'd previously set aside). When the time came to look at her application, one thing stood out immediately. It was her rental history. Sure enough, her rental history was full of different placed she'd live for less than 6 months! My hunch about her complaining was verified on the very first filter.

Now, quite a few landlords would probably catch this, but sadly many wouldn't. I mean, look at her previous rental history. It was full of former landlords who probably were disappointed they didn't research this tenant more.

I was happy to catch a bad tenant right away. I simply moved on and let the marketing system do its thing. I knew there would be more prospects calling my *Grasshopper* system soon.

Not long after I disqualified the first lady, another prospect came along for a showing. She initially seemed good, and she filled out an application form after viewing the property. My first impression was solid after reviewing the application, as her income was strong and there were no immediate red flags, so I continued on with the process.

She'd passed the application inspection, so it was time to check references. As always I cross-referenced the work phone number provided with the name of the company listed, which in this case was supposed to be a hair salon.

I found immediately that the phone number the prospect gave me belonged to a personal address. This didn't make sense, so I googled the name of the hair salon mentioned and found a different phone number. I called this number, and asked about the prospect. Sure enough, they had never heard of the prospect.

Alarm bells went off. This is a perfect example of a 3 percenter. She felt they needed to lie to get approved to live in the property. This is a big warning sign. Remember how I thought her income was strong? I had to throw that away. It was likely a lie, too. Immediately, I disqualified the tenant. As always, I didn't give her a specific reason. Her response was priceless. She was livid with me, demanding to know why I wouldn't let her move in. Her reaction confirmed my decision again.

It was back to the drawing board for me.

The next prospect that came along was a young couple. As always, I followed each step of the process. They kept passing steps, so I finally did a credit check on them. Luckily, I knew better than to spend the money on a credit check for the previous suspects, as they hadn't made it through the previous filters yet.

The young couple passed the credit check with flying colours, and after doing every single step of the system (which you've just read about in this book) I finally put them in the property. They lived up to their promise as excellent tenants, as they ended up living in the property for 3 years without making a mess, causing any trouble, or even bothering me, really. In fact, they even fixed a dishwasher and steam-cleaned the carpets. They were amazing.

These are the kind of tenants that make your life easy and put money in your pocket. I was thrilled with them, and about a year later I took a moment to reflect on what could have been. I had two chances to put a bad tenant into the property, but both of them were caught in the filtration system. As I thought about this I had a moment of clarity.

"No wonder so many landlords hate this business. If they're not catching the bad eggs, this could be an unpleasant job."

The landlording system makes all the difference in the real estate investment game. It's the difference between having staying power (and therefore making money) and having a terrible time (and therefore getting fatigued) and dropping out before the real profits arrive.

IN CONCLUSION

This book will guide you step-by-step through the process of filling a vacancy at your residential rental property. It really is the first part, of a two-part process. The second part, is managing that asset so that it continues to make you money, day after day, year after year, decade after decade. If you haven't already done so, I suggest that you pick-up a copy of my other book "*The Property Management Toolbox: A How-To Guide for Ontario Real Estate Investors and Landlords*" at www.TheOntarioLandlordToolbox.com, which explains how to do this with the proper processes and systems that will help to save you time and money.

Investing in residential real estate is simple, but it is not easy. You can help yourself to succeed by surrounding yourself with people who have similar goals and are also investing in residential real estate. I suggest that you find a local real estate club, like the Durham Real Estate

Investment Club (www.DurhamREI.ca), and grow your network. As the saying goes, your network is equal to your net worth. Build the network of people that you can go to in order to get support, then watch your net worth increase.

THE BIG PICTURE – OVERVIEW OF A VACANCY

Section 1

1. **Tenant Gives Notice to Vacate**
   - Tenant should give you minimum **60 days** notice. If the timeline is tighter follow the same steps in the system. Do not skip any steps.
   - **Tenant Breaking the Lease** - Give Letter Around Tenant Breaking The Lease or Negotiate a Break Fee

2. **Review Red Folder**
   - Review lease
   - Review pictures
   - Review move-in inspection form
   - Review ALL correspondence

2. **Make Appointment and View Property**
    *   View immediately
    *   Provide proper notice to view property using the <u>Notice to Enter Premises document</u>

5. **Provide Tenant with Move-Out Forms**
    *   Copy of lease (from Red Folder)
    *   <u>Accommodation Inspection Report Form</u>
    *   <u>Tenant Move Out Clean Up Checklist Form</u>
    *   <u>Tenant Utilities Info Release Form</u>

4. **Complete Tenant Exit Questionnaire**
    *   Complete an exit interview with the tenant to determine the following
    *   information about the property
    *   referrals for next tenants
    *   their next steps
    *   can you solve their issue? you can save the tenancy with this
    *   move to another one of your places?
    *   referral to another landlord, if they're going somewhere else

5. **Assess Property Condition**
    *   Take photos
    *   Make notes of obvious deficiencies
    *   Some work could be completed while the tenant is still there

6. **Rent Ready Checklist**

- Use the <u>Renovation Rent Ready Checklist Form</u>
- If renovation is required, go to <u>step 10</u>.

Section 2

8. Renovation Work Required

- Follow Renovation System
- Do not overdo Renovations

9. Line Up Team

- Send rent ready checklist to Property Maintenance Team
- Renovation Team
- Cleaning Team

10. Rent Ready?

11. If "Cleaning Only" Required

- <u>Cleaning Agreement Form</u>

12. Pre Book Appointments

- Call tenants and prebook times for potential showings or preliminary renovations using <u>Notice to Enter Premises document</u>

Section 3

13. Rental Comparables Worksheet

- Offline (newspapers)
- Online rental sites
- Google searches
- <u>Rentometer</u>
- <u>Rental Comparables Worksheet Form</u>

Section 4

14. Marketing System
- Create your marketing for the Vacancy
- Set yourself apart

15. Marketing 3 P's Reminder
- **Product**
- Quality of unit VS comparables
- Market Niche (i.e. pets, furnished, etc.)
- Unique Selling Proposition

- **Price**
- Premium/Over Market?
- Discount?
- Rebates?

- **Promotion**
- Advertising?
- Promotion?
- Publicity?

19. Media Sources
- **Online**
- rentfaster.ca
- rentboard.ca
- gottarent
- homerent
- kijiji
- craigslist

- facebook
- myREINspace

- **Property and Area**
- signs in windows and lawn
- directional signs
- flyers
- signs in local shops
- posters with numbers

- **Offline**
- newspaper
- rental magazines
- referrals
- current tenants
- other tenants
- Referral Form

17. Message (Ad Development)
- Develop your ad

- **Unique Selling Propostion (USP)**
- What sets your property apart from the current rentals?

- **Headline(s)**
- Strong attention grabbing headlines
- "Need a quiet neighbourhood"

- **Ad Copy**
- Benefits laden marketing copy
- Easy to read
- Tell a story
- Call to "action"

18. **Generate Leads**
    - **Phone**
    - Let voicemail or live answering service filter out many of the prospects

    - **Email/Website**
    - Have auto responder emails help filter out people, or guide them to specific websites
    - Website will have an online application process

Section 5

19. **Filter System**
20. **Tenant Questions**
    - Tenant Interview Questions Form
21. **PreApplication**
    - in person
    - online
    - fax
    - Application For Rental Accommodation Form

22. Eliminate Suspects

23. Prospects

- Spend time with this group

24. Process Application

- **Previous Landlord Check**
- "I understand you have a suite for rent...", checks whether or not application gave a real old landlord, or just a friend...

- **Employment Check**
- Do they have a job
- Are they a good employee

25. Book appointment to view

- Meet tenant at property
- Prospective tenant must phone in advance to confirm appointment
- NO? Go back to step 19
- YES? Continue to step 26

Section 6

26. Conditional Acceptance

- continue marketing property until tenant moves in
- Last Month Rent Deposit
- deposit against first month's rent
- Residential Tenancy Addendum Agreement
- If they have pets, you'll want this signed

27. Credit Check
- tenant verification services
- rentcheckcorp

Section 7

28. Rent Talk with Tenant
29. Unconditional Acceptance
- the whole process you're in control
- equity building tenants

30. Collect Full Deposits
- **certified funds by cheque** check that utilities have been transferred to tenant
- provide receipt
- never give access before receipt of all money and transfer of utilities

31. Receive Signed Lease
- Lease Agreement Form

32. Information for Tenants from the LTB
- date and sign two copies

Section 8

33. Photos
- all rooms
- bathroom area **
- main traffic areas
- appliances/walls/cabinets/flooring
- have tenant in a few photos

- photo 'date stamp" on ***
- some people use video camera and new apps

34. Acknowledgement of Landlord Address Form

35. Phone Utilities to confirm Transfer before the key is given

36. Ask for Tenant Liability Insurance

37. Movein Inspection Checklist

- Accomodation Inspection Report Form
- make copies of completed forms for tenants
- start new **RED** folder

38. Tenant Moves In

39. Welcome Basket

- Small welcome basket to start your relationship off on the right foot

40. Review Property Manual with Tenant

- Set the ground rules for effective tenancies
- Tenant Policy Handout
- Provide copies of
- lease
- tenant moveout cleanup checklist
- any other agreements
- put in binder/manual

41. Celebrate

- Equity building tenant

RESOURCES AND APPENDICES

Stay Up To Date on Laws and Get Support

The Ontario Landlord Tenant Act is tilted in the tenant's favour. It's your job as a landlord and property manager to stay on top of new information. There are a few key websites that can provide you with support and information:

1. Landlord Self-Help Centre - http://www.landlordselfhelp.com/ - This a non-profit community legal clinic which supports Ontario's small-scale landlord community exclusively. You can call them during business hours for answers to specific questions.

2. Landlord and Tenant Board - http://www.ltb.gov.on.ca – This is the Ontario Landlord Tenant Board web site. You can call and ask customer service for information about the Residential Tenancies Act, but they will not give legal advice.

3. Residential Tenancies Act - http://www.elaws. gov.on.ca/html/statutes/english/elaws statutes 06r17 e.htm - Here you can find the text of the entire Residential Tenancies Act.

4. CanLII - http://canlii.ca/en/on/onltb/index. html - Searchable database of recent decisions from the Landlord Tenant Board. Reviewing these cases can be very helpful.

RECOMMENDED BOOKS

The Property Management Toolbox: A How-To Guide for Ontario Real Estate Investors and Landlords by Quentin D'Souza, Andrew Brennan, Jeff Woods

The Ultimate Wealth Strategy: Your Complete Guide to Buying, Fixing, Refinancing, and Renting Real Estate by Quentin D'Souza

More Than Cashflow: The Real Risks & Rewards of Profitable Real Estate Investing by Julie Broad

Influence: The Psychology of Persuasion by Robert Cialdini

The Checklist Manifesto: How to Get Things Right by Atul Gawande

From Renos to Riches: The Canadian Real Estate Investor's Guide to Practical and Profitable Renovations by Ian Szabo

AUTHOR BIOGRAPHY – QUENTIN D'SOUZA

Quentin D'Souza is a highly respected multiple award winning Real Estate Investor in the Ontario Real Estate Investing community. He has appeared in, and been quoted in, many different real estate publications and books.

Quentin is a trusted authority on the Durham Real Estate Market and has worked with and mentored thousands of Real Estate Investors through the Durham Real Estate Investor Club (www.DurhamREI.ca) since 2008.

Quentin is also the author of *The Property Management Toolbox: A How-To Guide for Ontario Real Estate Investors and Landlords* (www.TheOntarioLandlordToolbox.ca), which is a comprehensive guide for getting a real estate business going. He is a co-author of *The Ultimate Wealth Strategy: Your Complete Guide to Buying, Fixing, Refinancing, and Renting Real Estate* (www.TheUltimateWealthStrategy.com) which shares his strategy for building a real estate portfolio.

Quentin manages a large real estate portfolio and works with other investors using joint ventures through his company Appleridge Homes (www.AppleridgeHomes.ca).

Quentin can often be found at one of his two sons' sports events or activities. When you see him in the community, please introduce yourself.

CPSIA information can be obtained
at www.ICGtesting.com
Printed in the USA
LVOW13s1252230917
549813LV00009B/565/P